CASH MONEY FREELANCING

Cash Money Freelancing:
76 bright ideas to make more money from your freelance business

Written by Tom Albrighton (abccopywriting.com)
Cover design by Andy Carolan (andycarolan.co.uk)
Editorial support by Liz Jones (ljed.co.uk)

Text and design © ABC Business Communications Ltd 2020.
All rights reserved. The moral right of the author has been asserted.

Apart from any fair dealing for the purposes of research of private study, or criticism or review, as permitted under the Copyright, Designs and Patents Act 1988, this publication may only be reproduced, stored or transmitted, in any form or by any means, with the prior permission of the publishers, or in the case of reprographic reproduction in accordance with the terms of licences issued by the Copyright Licensing Agency. Enquiries concerning reproduction outside those terms should be sent to the publisher.

ABC Business Communications Ltd accepts no responsibility or liability for any financial, marketing or business decision a reader may make, or refrain from making, based on the content of this book.

All URLs were correct at the time of publication, but online content may have been moved, changed or deleted since then. The author and publisher accept no responsibility for the content of third-party websites.

ABC

ABC Business Communications Ltd
100, George Borrow Road
Norwich NR4 7HU
United Kingdom

Email: info@abccopywriting.com
Web: www.abccopywriting.com

ISBN 978-1-8380545-5-7 (paperback)
ISBN 978-1-8380545-6-4 (hardback)

CASH MONEY FREELANCING

76 BRIGHT IDEAS TO MAKE MORE MONEY FROM YOUR FREELANCE BUSINESS

Contents

1 ON WORK, WEALTH AND MONEY MIND 1

2 SETTING DIRECTION 13
1. Know your purpose 13
2. Visualize your future 15
3. Know your ideal client 15
4. Know your unique value 17
5. Distinguish content from context 20
6. Set an earnings target 23
7. Disregard salaries 24
8. Forget your past 25
9. Aim for the top 26
10. Build a financial cushion 27
11. Put your cushion in context 28

3 SETTING YOUR PRICES 31
12. Charge by the project 31
13. Don't charge by time 32
14. Consider every factor 36
15. Set profitable precedents 38
16. Charge for everything 40
17. Charge for meetings 40
18. Charge for site visits 42
19. Charge for research 43
20. Charge for thinking 43
21. Charge for writing supporting notes 45
22. Charge for managing the project 47
23. Charge for changes 49
24. Charge for extras 51
25. Point out extras without charging 53
26. Charge for 'just having a look' 54
27. Charge for late payment 55

4 PRESENTING YOUR PRICES 59
28. Frame every price 59
29. Ask relevant questions, if you can 60
30. Write a detailed proposal 63
31. Itemize costs as well as tasks 65
32. Develop proposal modules and information sheets 66
33. Charge for proposals 66

5 NEGOTIATING DEALS 69
34. Stay frosty 69
35. Set your topline 70
36. Set your baseline 72
37. Express your price firmly 74
38. Know your BATNA 74

39	Know your prospect's BATNA	76
40	Don't play pipeline	78
41	Do paid samples, not free ones	80
42	Trade time for money	81
43	Trade money for time	82
44	Trade money for convenience	83
45	Reduce scope, not price	85
46	Use anchoring	86
47	Don't split the difference	88
48	Use bigness bias	90
49	Put your price in context	91
50	Act as if	92
51	Use 'feel, felt, found'	94
52	Walk away	95

6 INCREASING YOUR PRICES 99

53	Don't work more, charge more	99
54	Charge new clients more	100
55	Increase prices for existing clients	102
56	Think through what could happen	104
57	Record what you charge	107
58	Push past your own precedents	109
59	Keep up with inflation	110
60	Double your prices (or just think about it)	111
61	Increase your earnings target	113

7 BEING BUSINESSLIKE 117

62	Think business	117
63	Brand yourself	119
64	Build service packages	123
65	Offer a package menu	126
66	Work on retainer	129
67	Sell service subscriptions	131
68	Buddy up	132
69	Delegate	135
70	Specialize	139
71	Semi-specialize	142
72	Generalize	143
73	Diversify	144
74	Teach	149
75	Move along the value chain	152
76	Offer mini consultancy sessions	155

8 HOW MUCH IS ENOUGH? 159

1 ON WORK, WEALTH AND MONEY MIND

So, you've gone freelance. And you're making a living. But have you made yourself a life?

There's no doubt about it. Freelancing can be a wonderful way to work.

You can break free of the nine-to-five. You can get out from under the thumb of a controlling boss. You can create your own workspace, prioritize your own workload and manage your own time.

It should be liberating. But for some freelancers, it's more like a prison sentence.

They've got the skills, they've got the work and they've got the clients. But their freelance life still doesn't add up. For them, it seems there isn't that much 'free' in freelancing after all.

The reason? They simply don't make enough money.

What is true wealth?

We all want to do work we love. But however much you enjoy your work, you still wouldn't do it for fun. At the end of the day, you work to get money. You only have so many hours to spend on this earth, and if you choose to spend them working, you should be well rewarded for doing so.

At the most basic level, you need money to live. Beyond that threshold, you want money so you can buy and do more of the things you like, and avoid the things you don't. In this sense, more money makes you happier.

However, life isn't just about money, and merely having money will never bring you true happiness. What will truly make you happy is *wealth*.

Money represents power and potential. But it doesn't mean anything until you actually use it. You can use it positively, to create the life you want. Or you can use it negatively – for example, by accumulating and hoarding cash for its own sake, or spending it ostentatiously, purely to prove a point to others.

While money is just a number on a screen, true wealth is a *state of being*. It's about using money to buy the experiences that bring pleasure and meaning to your life. Those experiences are different for everyone. But for most of us, they're in areas like travel, home, spirit, nature, sport or culture, and they often involve spending time with family, friends or loved ones.

From this perspective, you can see that wealth doesn't necessarily mean having loads of money, because the things you want might not even be that expensive. You might 'pay' for them in time or commitment, as well as cash.

But whatever your goals are, none of them can happen unless you have the time and opportunity to pursue them. And money gives you that choice. When you have it, you can reclaim your time from work, so you can spend it doing other things that have more value for you.

To sum up so far: the more money you make, the more time you can spend doing the things you love. And that is the true meaning of wealth.

So, ask yourself – and answer honestly. Is your freelance work bringing you the wealth you want?

If not, it's time to make a change. And that's precisely what this book will help you do.

Money mind, and why you need it

When you go freelance, you begin selling your skills on the open market. So whatever abilities you have – and I'm sure you have plenty – you must also know how to turn those abilities into cash. Otherwise, it doesn't matter how good you are; your talent will wither on the vine.

Every business exists to create and capture value. Firms create value for their customers in the form of products and services. And they also capture value for themselves, mainly in the form of money. As long as a firm can continue to create and capture value, it's a going concern.

Freelancing is just the same. You need to create value for your clients with your skills, and you need to capture value in return. As long as you can do that, you've got a viable freelance business.

However, unlike a large corporation, you don't have a production department and a sales department. You don't even have an operations director and a marketing director. You're just one person, making all the decisions on your own. And yet, you must still ensure that your freelance business can create and capture value.

That's why you need a 'money mind' to sit alongside your 'work mind'. In other words, you need a part of yourself – call it a mindset, an attitude or whatever – that's completely focused on the commercial side of your freelancing.

Work mind is about creating value, while money mind is about capturing it. While your work mind is busy serving in the shop out front, your money mind is taking care of business in the back office. Together, they make sure your freelance business is doing everything that it should.

Your money mind is active rather than passive; conscious rather than unconscious. With your money mind, you take full responsibility for your freelance business, and make purposeful choices to develop it in new and profitable ways. It's the missing link from your work to your wealth.

Money mind is not about making a big resolution, a grand gesture or a one-off effort. It's something you cultivate over time. It's about making many small decisions, every day, so you can take every opportunity to increase your wealth.

Often, money mind is about breaking habits that you may have learned long ago, and continue to follow without even being aware of them. You may even regard them as immutable character traits, although you're always free to change them. Money mind opens the door to a different path. It gets in between your work and your habitual reactions to speak up on behalf of your wallet.

As you break old habits, so you can create new ones. The more money-mind decisions you make, the easier it is to make more decisions along the same lines. And the more you practise your new habits, the more natural they will feel.

Work is not enough

Freelancers run into money problems when they don't have their work mind and money mind in balance. That might be because they focus too much on work mind, or because they neglect money mind, or both. Let's consider why that happens.

For some freelancers, it's all about the work. They just want to spend as much time as possible doing the activity they most enjoy. They didn't go freelance to think about money all day, or to tie themselves up in red tape. In fact, they probably started freelancing precisely so they could get away from corporate suits and the bean-counters from accounting.

Unfortunately, it's not that simple.

Yes, it would be wonderful if you could focus on doing the work you love, and money just magically appeared. Maybe it really does work out that way, for a few lucky freelancers. But for the rest of us, wealth is not like sunshine, which will surely appear if you wait long enough. Instead, it's something you have to make happen for yourself.

That's why merely being good at what you do is not enough. It's necessary, but it's not sufficient. It will get you on the road, but it won't take you all the way to your destination.

'Just do the work' is the motto of an employee – and a naïve one at that. It's what people tell themselves when they're hoping that their boss will notice what they do and reward them with a pay rise. It's not the mindset of someone who creates, owns and manages a business for themselves.

Two minds, one purpose

The important thing to remember is that your money mind and your work mind are not enemies. They work in harmony, not opposition. Cultivating your money mind doesn't take anything away from your work mind. In fact, they reinforce each other.

Consider what happens if you neglect money mind and focus purely on the work. The only way to earn more is to work more. You may feel you have to take every job, or spend all your time working, or cut corners on one job so you can squeeze in another. That means you wind up doing lower-quality work, and probably burning yourself out too. You are in a race to the bottom, in every sense.

Now see how things change when money mind enters the picture. You make a conscious effort to bring in better-paying clients, generate higher fees and explore new ways to develop your business. You're still working hard *in* your business, but you're working hard *on* your business too.

As your earnings grow, you can be more selective about which jobs you take on. Then you can take your time to deliver high-quality work on every job, and for every client. And you can make sure you stay physically and mentally healthy, so you can sustain your success into the future.

So while doing great work brings you more money, earning more money also enables you to do great work. Money mind and work mind combine to improve your freelancing life in every aspect: the work you do, the money you make and the wealth you enjoy. It's a positive – and profitable – feedback loop.

You don't have to stop being you

Now, you might already be thinking that you don't like the sound of money mind. Maybe it sounds like someone you wouldn't really warm to, if you met them.

That's why some freelancers shy away from the whole idea of money mind. They feel it's just not them, or that money mind is incompatible with their character.

Other freelancers might avoid money mind because they feel it doesn't fit with their values. They see money mind as something acquisitive, materialistic or entrepreneurial, and they're just not that kind of person. So to them, focusing on money just doesn't feel right. They'd rather someone else took care of all that.

But cultivating a money mind *doesn't* mean becoming a different person. Whatever you choose to do in your freelance business, you are still you.

You don't have to transform your personality overnight, or force yourself to think and act in some alien way. You don't have to toss your principles overboard or torch your values. You just have to think certain thoughts and take certain actions at certain times, so you can step on to a different path. That's all.

Think of money mind as a pair of glasses that you put on to do a certain job, then take off again when you're done. You need your money perspective at certain times, but that doesn't mean you have to permanently change the way you see the world.

That goes for me too! I'm not a pushy or aggressive person, either in my business or in any other part of my life. I've even written a whole book about freelancing as an introvert.

Actually, having that sort of personality was the cue for me to change my thinking about money. I realized that if I relied on my natural character to guide me in every aspect of my work, I'd wind up being paid less than I was worth. So I decided to cultivate my own money mind. And as a result, I got to work the way I want and do the things I enjoy.

Just as money mind stands guard over the quality of your work, so it also protects the core of your character. You step into money mind to sort out your money, and you come out again to do everything else. You take care of your business so it can take care of you – but it still stays in its box, and it doesn't spread into every area of your life.

What are you afraid of?

That may sound like a taunt or a challenge, but it's not. It's a constructive suggestion to take an honest look at what's going on inside your head.

Task focus, innate character and firm principles may all sound like plausible reasons for avoiding money mind. But maybe they all boil down to something far deeper and more powerful.

Fear.

When we're honest with ourselves, a lot of our reasons for not acting are really fears disguised as character traits, values or ideas. And whatever tale we tell ourselves, it's actually the fear that came first. Our rationalizations are just words that we piled on top of our negative emotions so we didn't have to feel them any more.

For freelancers, there could be several different types of fear at play.

First of all, we all feel anxious about change. That's completely natural. It's only human to prefer the known and familiar to the unknown and the strange. If money mind feels alien to you, taking on these new ways of thinking can be unnerving.

But if you keep on doing what you've always done, you'll just get more of what you've always got. So if what you have now isn't working for you, you *have* to look for something new – even if it brings you some discomfort in the short term.

Other freelancers might be anxious that their clients will be upset or offended by higher rates. They might even feel that by asking for more money, they're somehow taking advantage of their clients.

If you think this, remember that money mind is only about getting paid what you're worth. It's not about extorting or blackmailing money out of innocent victims. It's about getting the money that is *already* due to you – money that you've been leaving on the table until now.

What's more, clients only use you because they want to. Every business deal is freely entered into by both parties. You are absolutely free to set your terms, and your clients are free to take them or leave them, as they wish. All you're going to do is decide what you want, say it out loud and wait for an answer.

Another important lesson is that actions have consequences. If you want to make more money from freelancing, you have to accept that some clients might move on, or that you won't necessarily win every job. Selecting clients can be just as important as attracting them. Achieving wealth isn't just about 'more' – it's about 'different' and 'better' too.

Finally, some freelancers might worry about what other people will think of them if they suddenly start acting like a boss. But in my experience, your friends and family are more likely to be impressed, if not actually envious. Besides, most of your money dealings remain completely private, between you and the client alone. No one need ever know what a badass you've become.

If you're feeling any of these fears, try thinking of it this way. You can have what you want, or you can have your reasons for not having it. The choice is yours.

Time to choose

When you go freelance, your fate is in your hands, and yours alone. No one is coming to the rescue. Very few clients will offer you more money than you ask for, no matter how deeply they value what you do. So if you want rewards, you have to hustle for them. That is an unchangeable truth of freelance life.

Basically, if you're doing tons of great work for loads of great clients, but your freelance life still isn't coming together, money mind is the missing piece of the puzzle. It will bring you the freelance life you've always wanted, and *knew* was out there somewhere, but still could never quite reach.

Once upon a time, I was exactly where you are now. I was making an OK living from freelancing, but I wanted so much more. So I made a conscious decision to do things differently.

Over the years, step by step, I took control of my freelance life. I realized that while money gives you more choice, some choices also bring you more money. I accepted that it was up to me to make a change. From there, I began learning how to make freelancing pay, and gradually built up a freelance business that hits six figures in the good years.

A few of my lessons came from reading books, or from talking to the business scholars I met through my academic editing work. Many came from conversations with my fellow freelancers. But most of them were gained through a long, hard process of learning, as I discovered through sheer trial and error what did and didn't work. And now they're yours.

About this book

As the title suggests, this book contains 76 ideas that you can use to make more money from your freelance business.

My own business is freelance writing and editing, but this book is for freelancers of every kind. No matter whether you're a party planner or a pet groomer, a financial planner or a fitness instructor, you'll find ideas here that will work for you.

Now, some of the ideas might take a while to fall into place for you. Some might not feel right, and some might not work with your individual business. But with so many ideas to choose from, I'm confident you'll find plenty of knowledge here that you can pick up and adapt to your situation.

The 76 ideas are grouped into six chapters, each on a different theme:

- In chapter 2, we'll start with the *basics*: setting targets and understanding the unique value you offer.
- In chapters 3 and 4, we'll move on to how you *set prices* and *present them* to your prospects.[1]
- In chapter 5, we'll look at *negotiation* – ways to reach an agreement if your prospect doesn't agree to your proposal straight away. You might find these ideas useful in other areas of life too.
- In chapter 6, we'll talk about ways to *increase your prices*, from simply keeping pace with inflation to doubling your rates overnight.
- In chapter 7, we'll explore further afield, with ideas to make your freelance business more *entrepreneurial*.
- In the final chapter, we'll circle back to the points in this introduction, but with a new perspective based in money mind.

However you use this book, I hope you find it helpful, and I hope your freelancing brings you the wealth you want – whatever wealth means to you.

Now, let's make a start.

---

[1] Throughout this book, I use the word 'prospect' to describe a person or business who is considering using your service, and 'client' to describe someone who is actually using it, or has used it at some point in the past. So a prospect becomes a client once they decide to buy from you.

2 SETTING DIRECTION

'Anywhere but here' is not a useful destination. So don't begin your wealth journey without a clear sense of where you're going.

1 Know your purpose

'Everybody loves money,' says Danny DeVito in *Heist*. 'That's why they call it money.'

It's true. Everybody *does* love money. You obviously do, or you wouldn't be reading this. But as we saw in chapter 1, what you really love is *what money can get you*, or what money *allows you to do*. That's the true meaning of wealth.

Business guru Simon Sinek advises firms to 'start with why'. In other words, they need to define their *purpose* before they rush into making plans, developing products and finding customers. Without that basic sense of direction, those other activities will lack meaning and context.

So before you go out looking to make money, ask yourself this question: What do you want money *for?* What gets you out of bed in the morning? What keeps you moving forward?

It could be to have nice things. It could be to make yourself more secure, or to create a better future for yourself. It could be to support your family, or improve their lifestyle. It could be to have more time to do the things you want, or pursue your interests. And it could be a combination of all these things.

Often, the things that really make us happy are *experiences* rather than possessions. That's why our memories of vacations, reunions or celebrations stay bright and vivid for the whole of our lives, while prized possessions become faded and forgotten.

However, experiences always have a physical side, and many material possessions have an experiential aspect to them. For example, if you buy an expensive bike or camera that you never use, purely to impress other people, that is not a great use of your money. (In fact, you're actually using your money to *destroy* your wealth, because you're denying yourself the chance to do other, more fulfilling things.)

However, if you buy a bike to train for a 100-mile ride, or an SLR camera to capture the perfect image of an eagle, that's more than mere material acquisition. It's about achieving your goals. The tangible possession is just a means to an end.

As you can see, you don't have to be on a mission to change the world. Once our basic needs are taken care of, most of us work so we can have more of the stuff we like, and less of the stuff we don't. But it's usually best to have some element of helping others in there – even if it's only to support those close to you. Our lives are most meaningful in relation to other people.

Why is it so important to have a purpose? Because researchers have found that, beyond a certain point, gaining more money doesn't actually make us any happier.[2] If you keep on seeking material riches after that point, you'll find that you need more and

---

[2] Bryan Forbes, 'No, A Pay Raise Won't Make You Happier', *Forbes*, 27 December 2018.

more money to gain less and less happiness. An economist might say that you are facing *diminishing marginal utility*.

So, before you get stuck in a hamster wheel of money-chasing, get clear in your mind why you're climbing on to it in the first place.

2 Visualize your future

Before you begin any journey, you need to know where you're going. And freelancing is just the same.

To create your own roadmap for the future, write down a vision of what you want from your freelance life.

Your vision can cover every aspect of your work – your services, your clients, your workspace, your day-to-day working style. It can also cover what you want outside work – your leisure time, your family plans, your retirement. And, crucially, it can cover money – how much you want, where you'll get it and what you want it for.

I'm not setting you this writing exercise just to make you feel you've done something concrete. Writing things down has an awesome power. It gives your mind something solid and vivid to aim for, and mobilizes your mental resources towards making it real.

So commit your vision to paper, and keep it somewhere safe. Then, later on, don't be too surprised when you notice it start to come true.

3 Know your ideal client

If I told you to work for the right clients, you might say my advice was fairly obvious. But the truth is that many freelancers are far too passive about their client base. They prefer to work for whoever knocks on their door, rather than making conscious decisions and seeking out the clients who are best for them.

At the very least, you should spend some time thinking about the profile of your ideal client. It will help you identify the most promising new-business prospects to approach – or, when you receive approaches, to direct your attention and energy towards the most promising ones.

Even if you don't do that much proactive marketing, and rely on referrals, it's still worth having a sense of who you ideally want to work with. It will help to prepare your mind and guide your actions in the right way. If you believe in the law of attraction (as I do), then just thinking about your ideal client will help to bring them into your life.

So, what actually makes a good client?

I suggest that your ideal client is one who meets the BAR. The acronym stands for three essential attributes, summarized as Benefits, Appreciation and Resources:

1. The client *benefits* significantly from the unique value you offer. Whatever you do for them, it makes a big difference to their business or their life. That can mean tangible things like business success, quicker results or financial savings, but also intangible, emotional factors like reassurance and self-esteem.

2. The client *appreciates* the unique value you offer them. No matter how valuable your work is in reality, it's hard to price it right if people can't really see how it helps them. Of course, they can always learn that, and you can teach them – but your best clients will be the ones who know it already.

3. The client has enough *resources* to pay you at the level you want. Now, this can be tough, because it might rule out clients who score highly on the first two points. For example,

a start-up firm might be crazy about your web design skills, and desperate for a great website – but if they're chronically short of cash and at constant risk of going under, you may still need to steer clear.

I'm not necessarily saying you should turn down every new prospect who falls short of the BAR, or (more radically) fire those current clients who don't meet it. Rather, you should just keep the BAR in mind as you make decisions relating to clients – which ones to go the extra mile for, which ones to go and meet and so on. The basic idea is to direct your efforts where they'll have the most results.

Once you know who your ideal clients are, you can go out and find them. Use Google, business directories and sites like LinkedIn to make a list of high-value prospects to approach, then send them a tailored letter or email introducing your service. To make your approach effective, you need to explain your unique value and link it to the client's context. So let's look at both of those things now.

4 Know your unique value

When a restaurant puts a pizza on the menu for £15, they're not charging that for some bread, tomato and cheese. In fact, the ingredients of the dish probably cost less than £2.

Instead, that's what you pay to have your pizza expertly cooked to order and brought to your table by a polite server, then eat it at a leisurely pace, in pleasant surroundings, and leave without clearing up.

All those things come together to form an overall experience that has a certain appeal for you. In other words, the price reflects the *unique value* you get from what you're buying – not just the various elements that go into it.

The point about unique value is that it's worth whatever the buyer is willing to pay. If you want the experience of going to that particular pizza restaurant, you have no choice but to pay the price on the menu. If you want an experience that's similar but not quite the same, you might be able to get it slightly cheaper elsewhere. And if you're happy with a frozen pizza stuck in the microwave, you can pay a third of the price, stay at home and cook it yourself.

In the same way, your freelance service offers a unique blend of value. It flows from your skills, your experience (both in your work and outside it), your approach and your personality.

For clients, your unique value includes all the benefits they get from your work, both tangible and intangible. Those benefits might be anything from high-level business outcomes like increased sales or profits through to personal goals such as better physical fitness, and emotional states such as confidence or security. They also include the experience of working with you, as distinct from the actual service you provide.

To understand the value you offer, consider all the possible answers to the question, 'How do you help your clients?'

For example, you could ask yourself:

- What *goals* do you help your clients to reach?
- What *outcomes* do you help them to achieve?
- How do you help your clients *make money*, or *save money*? How do you help them *save time*?
- What *problems do you solve* for your clients?
- What *tasks* do you take on, or make easier? What would your clients have to do if they *didn't* use you?

- What *knowledge*, *insight* or *understanding* do you offer to your clients? What unique *perspectives* can you bring to their business, their life or their work?

- How are your *clients' lives improved* as a result of your work? How might they *feel differently* after working with you?

- How do your own *character traits* – including those that are sometimes seen as negative – strengthen your service? For example, why is it good for clients that you're an introverted writer, a control-freak event manager, a perfectionist web developer or a daydreamy illustrator?

- What distinctive *experiences* do you bring to your work? In other words, how do the things you've *seen and done* help clients?

- How does your *identity* influence your work? In other words, how does *who you are* help clients? Why is it good for them to work with someone like you? This could include things like your age, gender, sexual orientation, race, cultural background, physical ability and so on.

- What do clients *enjoy* about working with you? What parts of the process do they particularly like?

All these things come together to form a unique blend of value that your clients can't get anywhere else. You may not think of all the 'softer' factors as important parts of what you do, but from the client's perspective, they can all add value – and your fee should reflect that. Don't put a supermarket price tag on a restaurant experience.

If you're having trouble with the questions above, try talking to your clients. Ask them why they chose you, and what they value most about your service. The answers might surprise you – and boost your confidence too.

Unique value is why freelancers are able to keep their clients' loyalty, year after year. Once clients know and appreciate what you do, they generally won't look elsewhere unless they have a good reason to do so. In the same way that you keep going back to your favourite restaurant because it's just right for you, so clients keep coming back because your unique value is just right for them.

As you move through your freelance career, you're bound to compare yourself with other freelancers – and that can be a recipe for anxiety. So remember: even if they offer a service that seems to be similar or even superior to yours on paper, they're still not you! Whatever they may have going on in terms of skills, experience, clients, portfolio, social-media presence, age, character or even personal appeal, the experience of using them will never be the same as working with you. Clients *will* value your service, and they'll pay for it too. All you have to do is find them.

5 Distinguish content from context

Another useful perspective on your unique value is content versus context. The *content* of your work is what you actually do for your clients: the tasks you carry out, or the things you deliver. The *context* is how clients use your work, or what it enables them to do.

In the analogy of the pizza restaurant I used above, the content is things like the taste of the toppings, the smile of the server or the cleanliness of the cutlery. But the *context* for those things might be a couple's first date, a retirement celebration or a child's birthday party. The people involved in those occasions don't care that much about little details in themselves. They only care how they affect the overall experience.

Now, the restaurant can't do anything about the context. That's beyond their control. All they can do is get the content right. But by focusing on the tangible side of the experience, the restaurant enables high-level intangible benefits for its patrons: a second date, a precious memory or a happy child. Those are things that the customers only get one chance to get right, and they will happily pay for.

Think about the context of your own freelance work. Ask yourself questions such as:

- What *situation* will your clients be in when they use you? What events might have happened that would prompt them to get in touch?

- What *concerns* will your clients have? What will be keeping them awake at night?

- What is *at risk* for the client in relation to your work? How do they stand to lose time, money, reputation, opportunity or anything else? Once lost, could it be regained?

- What important things do you help your clients *get right first time*? What would be the implications for them if they got those things wrong, and had to correct them? Would they be able to correct them at all?

- How will your work be *used* from now on? And how long for? For example, if you're designing a letterhead for a business, they might use it as a basis for all their client communications for a decade or more.

- What other things or people *depend on your work*? How does your work enable other things to happen, or allow other people to do their jobs?

- What *other people* might have a stake in the outcome of your work? For example, if you work for businesses, your contact might be anxious to impress their boss. Or, if you take wedding photos, the happy couple need images they'll be happy to share with their guests.

Understanding the context of your work is a useful foundation for other techniques we'll explore later in the book. For example, it can help you increase your prices (chapter 6) or explore new avenues like branding yourself and moving along the value chain (chapter 7).

Context should also be the basis for your approaches to potential new clients. Instead of starting from what you want to say, and the outcome you want, start from where the prospect is now. Talk about their situation, their concerns and their priorities. Mention problems they might have, and how you can help to solve them.

When you appreciate context, you also get a valuable insight into your clients' behaviour. Yes, there are a handful of clients who will try to gain power over you, or seem to actively enjoy messing you around. But most of them just want to get something done or make something happen. The more the client has invested in that outcome – financially, professionally or personally – the more they may come across as fussy or over-controlling, when in fact they're just anxious about everything turning out right.

While the client is talking to you about the content of your work, what they're really worried about is their own context. That is the source of their thoughts, feelings, words and actions. They are trying to influence their context through the only means available to them right now: the content of your work. So if you feel that they're treading on your toes, try walking in their shoes.

Once you understand them, you'll be in a better position to offer them the reassurance they need.

To understand your clients' context, just talk to them. Without being too intrusive, ask them about some of the areas above. You might find that they're delighted to have a sympathetic listener who understands exactly what they're going through. And once you've established this rapport, it can be a vital part of the unique value you offer them.

At the other end of the scale, some prospects may adopt the aggressive and reductive strategy of denying context completely and focusing exclusively on content instead. For example, they might ask something like, 'Why does it cost so much just for a few words on a website?' Since they don't appreciate your value, they don't reach the BAR – and it's probably not worth the trouble of enlightening them.

6 Set an earnings target

Now you know who you want to work for, and the unique value you offer, set a target for how much you want to earn.

Set your earnings target according to the 'Three As':

- *Ambitious.* Your target should be stretching. That probably means more than you've ever earned before, although you could be aiming to regain a previous peak. When you think about this target, you should feel a touch of doubt over whether you could actually reach it – but a shiver of excitement at the thought that you could.
- *Achievable.* At the same time, your target shouldn't be a fantasy. It should be out of reach, but not out of sight. For example, you could aim for a level that you've heard the most

successful freelancers in your industry talk about. Or you could aim to double what you're earning right now.

- ***Absolute.*** Your target should be an absolute number with a fixed timescale, like '£50,000 in the next year'. Don't make it vague, relative or unbounded, like 'earn a bit more money in future'. The problem here is that £1 is 'more money'; the next five decades is 'in future'. Your mind needs something real and solid to get hold of; if you put uncertainty out, you'll get uncertainty back.

Annual earnings targets work best, because they match up with the natural timescale of accounting. Monthly billings are probably too up and down, plus you'll be hitting or missing your target so often that it will lose all meaning.

You could also express your goals in terms of clients or projects. For example, once you've worked out who your ideal clients are, you could set yourself a target of acquiring a certain number of them over the next year. Or you could aim to win a certain number of ideal projects, which will be those where you have most opportunity to offer your unique value.

7   Disregard salaries

Because accounts are usually filed on a yearly basis, most freelancers get used to thinking of earnings in terms of an annual 'salary', even though they aren't actually employed.

However, your target doesn't have to be linked to any particular salary. Specifically, it doesn't have to reflect what other people in similar roles earn through employment – because that isn't comparing like with like.

Remember, salaries only cover hands-on work. As a freelance business owner, your earnings have to cover *everything* –

equipment, supplies, premises, training, travel, insurance, tax *and* whatever you pay yourself. Plus you don't earn anything when you're off sick or taking a break, so your earnings have to cover that too.

In fact, it's better to think of your earnings as *turnover*, rather than salary. Your turnover is all the money you bring in, while your salary (or profit) is what's left when you've covered all your costs. This is part of thinking of yourself as a business – a theme we'll return to in chapter 7.

8   Forget your past

Just as you shouldn't link your target to other people's earnings, so you shouldn't base it on your own past earnings either.

If you were previously in employment, it's easy to think of your salary as 'what you can earn', or even 'what you're worth'. So you carry that forward into your freelancing and adopt it as a target, possibly without consciously thinking about it at all.

In fact, that number has very little to do with the value you create – and even less to do with your intrinsic worth. It's just the minimum your employer felt they had to pay you. In setting your salary, they might have been far more concerned with getting you on board, or keeping you loyal, than with actually recognizing and valuing your work.

We also know that employers can be wildly inconsistent in terms of what they pay. For example, they pay women less than men for doing the same work, or give rises to favoured employees to stop them leaving. Or, on the flip side, they may be happy to leave some people at pretty much the same level for years on end, as long as nobody complains.

Clearly, when it comes to salaries, fairness and objectivity aren't even in the frame. So there are plenty of reasons not to use them as a benchmark.

However, the same point also applies to your own freelance earnings. If you've been freelancing for a while, you might regard your past years' turnover as 'what you can earn'. After all, that's the price that the market has put on your work so far.

But while the numbers are real, that view of them is far too passive. It underestimates the power you have to change your situation.

When you think about it, freelance earnings come from within, as much as from without. What I mean is that even though the actual cash flows in from clients, the amount you earned comes from the expectations that *you* brought to the table in those years, which shaped your own actions when you were setting and agreeing prices. If your actions had been different, the outcome might have been different too. So while your earnings do reflect what clients paid, the more fundamental point is that they reflect what you asked for.

What I'm saying here is very simple: the future does *not* have to be like the past. Once you set new expectations, you can take new actions, and achieve different results.

9 Aim for the top

If you're unsure what earnings target to set, look for industry surveys and other publications that will tell you what people generally earn. Based on what you discover, set your target towards the top end of your industry, while still being realistic about your own age, skills and experience.

You can also look at posts and articles written by individual freelancers to get a sense of what people earn. However, there are three things to bear in mind.

First, the writers may be outliers within your industry – real 'stars' who can command exceptional fees because of their high profile. You can certainly aim to emulate them, but you need to be prepared to match their actions if you want to see the same results. Nobody gets to the top by accident.

Second, they may have an incentive to paint a rosy picture of their earnings – for example, because they're selling you a course. Nobody wants a teacher who can't walk the walk themselves.

Finally, remember that there's a difference between saying 'I charge X' and consistently pulling down that rate on every job. People might be talking a good game in public, but doing less lucrative deals behind the scenes.

10   Build a financial cushion

I'm sure you've seen this advice before – perhaps too many times. It can be irritating if you feel you're already saving all you can, or simply don't have cash to spare. But I still have to mention it here, because it's so vital to every freelance business.

As soon as you can, start saving part of your earnings to build up a financial 'cushion'. Open a separate savings account (perhaps alongside your company bank account) and set up a regular payment into it, however small. Then tell yourself you will only withdraw that cash if you absolutely have to (for example, to pay an annual tax bill).

The main function of your cushion is to protect you against the unexpected. If you hit a dry spell, it will keep the wolf from the door. Or if you need to make a big purchase, like a new vehicle, you can buy it right away, so your business doesn't miss a beat.

However, that's only one part of how a cushion helps. It also gives you a psychological foundation that supports many of the income-boosting ideas in this book. For example, when you know your cushion is there, it's easier to be firm about price increases (chapter 6) or adopt a strong stance in negotiations (chapter 5).

Moreover, if you do hit hard times, your cushion can save you from second-guessing clients by lowballing to win work. As we'll see in chapter 3, that's a recipe for disaster, because you set an unwanted precedent that could carry over into the good times when they return. With a cushion in place, it's far easier to avoid this kind of self-sabotage.

Obviously, what I'm describing here is a bit of a chicken-and-egg. The cushion will help you make money, but you need to make money in order to build it up in the first place. So for now, just set yourself the goal, open the account and start saving. Any effort is better than doing nothing at all, and you might be surprised at how quickly your cushion grows.

11 Put your cushion in context

As with other aspects of your wealth, it's helpful to think of your financial cushion in terms of the power it gives you, rather than just an abstract number on a bank statement.

For example, I think of my cushion in terms of how long I could go without work, if I had to. I know how much money I need to pay all my essential bills every month, so if I divide my cushion total by that amount, I get the number of months I can go without any income at all. If everything goes south, that's the time I will have to gain new clients, or even find some alternative form of work. It's good to know that, even if the worst comes to the worst, the wolf won't be right outside your door just yet.

Of course, it will almost certainly never come to that. Provided your freelance work is spread across multiple clients, it's hard to imagine a situation where you'd lose *all* of it in one go. More likely, you'll suffer a dry month, or a period where you're not quite at full capacity. In that situation, you'll just use your cushion to top up your earnings, sustaining you for even longer.

Another perspective on your cushion is as a resource that could fund some marketing or new-business initiatives to address your shortfall of work. For example, you could do some online advertising, or hire a virtual assistant to do some cold-calling on your behalf. Here, you're thinking of your cushion as a reservoir of potential action: a ready-made crisis response that you keep in your back pocket, ready to go.

Even when times are relatively good, you can bolster your confidence by comparing the value of freelance jobs that you're quoting for with your cushion. For example, you could think, 'OK, I'm going to quote £1000 for this project. I hope I get it – but if I don't, at least I know I've got my £5000 cushion to fall back on. In a way, I've got five jobs like this in the bank already.'

That perspective helps you in two ways. First, it gives you the inner resolve to quote at the right level, so you can act out of self-assurance rather than fear. And second, if you do miss out on the work, it helps you keep your loss in proportion. Yes, it would have been nice to get that job – but at least your financial foundation is intact. Another opportunity will surely come along, so you haven't really lost anything apart from time.

Takeaways from this chapter

- Vividly imagine your future so it's more likely to come true.
- Know your ideal client: you *benefit* them, they *appreciate* you and they have enough *resources*.

- Understand the unique value you offer, in all its dimensions, and the context of your work for the client.
- Set an ambitious but achievable earnings target. Don't be held back by what happened in the past.
- Build a financial cushion to support your success. See it in terms of time, opportunity and action, not just money.

3 SETTING YOUR PRICES

Setting prices is the first and most vital step towards making money from freelancing. This chapter outlines the key principles and explores some of the elements you can build into your price.

12 Charge by the project

The best way to reflect your unique value is to charge by the project, as opposed to charging by time or quantity.

With project-based charging, you quote a simple, flat fee for taking on the whole project, and make it very clear what that fee covers. We'll look at some of the tasks and elements you could charge for in the rest of this chapter.

The only real disadvantage of project-based pricing is that you must fully understand what the project will involve before you can set your price. That can make the quoting process longer and more complex than it might be otherwise.

However, I think that downside is far outweighed by the upsides of project-based pricing, which are:

- It's *simple* – one job, one fee. This simplicity encourages clients to accept the price at face value, rather than questioning how it's been arrived at. It is simply 'the price'.

- It's *predictable*. The price is set at the outset, and it doesn't change. That reduces uncertainty and risk for both sides.
- It's *fair*. Both sides agree what the job is worth and shake hands on it before work begins.
- It reflects *the value the client gets* from the project, not the time or effort you put into it. If your work makes the client's life easier, saves them time or helps their business to succeed, the price should reflect that.
- It *rewards you for quick work*. No matter how long it takes you to finish the work, you can still invoice for the same amount, and move on to a different project. Basically, you spend whatever time the project demands – *not* whatever hours you've quoted for.
- Unlike time-based pricing, it *frees up your earnings potential*. There's no limit to how much you can make, particularly if you're happy with charging different rates to different clients. (We'll come back to this later.)
- It's *consistent*. You can set prices for certain types of project that work for both sides, then stick to them over the long term. That's transparent for clients, saves time on the quoting process and brings stability to your earnings.

13 Don't charge by time

If you want to be rewarded for your unique value, don't just sell your time. In other words, don't use hourly or daily rates unless you have a good reason to do so.

Time is an input rather than an output. It only reflects what you put into a project – not the value that the client gets out of it. You are far more than just a hired hand.

One of the biggest disadvantages of time-based pricing is that it imposes an upper limit on your earnings. There are only so many hours in a day, or days in a year. So once you've determined your hourly or daily rate, you've also put a cap on the money you can make.

Prospects sometimes ask for time-based rates so they can make quick and easy comparisons between freelancers. The problem is that those comparisons are *too* quick and easy – because they don't take account of what the prospect will actually get for their money. Instead of looking at the unique value each freelancer can offer them, the prospect thinks of them as interchangeable commodities – as if hiring a freelancer was no different from buying a sack of flour. (It's the same mindset that leads some managers to refer to team members as 'resources', or even 'bodies'.)

This is why using time-based prices can often lead to unproductive conversations with clients. You can get bogged down in how long a project should take, or what a reasonable hourly rate should be – effectively, haggling over the price of a commodity.

For example, suppose you're a freelance writer, like me, and a prospect asks you to quote for writing an online article. If you tell them it will cost them £100, they have three choices: accept, decline or try to negotiate a different price (which we'll cover in chapter 5).

But what if you tell the prospect that you charge £50 per hour, and the job will take two hours? Financially, the deal is exactly the same. But now you've thrown two extra elements into the mix: first, how much you want to be paid per hour, and second, how long it will take you to do the work. And those are both things that your prospect simply doesn't need to know, or even think about. What happens behind the scenes is none of their business; they're here to see the show.

If you frame your price in terms of time, there's a risk that the prospect will question why the job should take that long, or whether you should be getting that much per hour, or both. They might ask why you can't match someone else's rate, or their time estimate. The whole discussion is deeply unproductive, and it just drags you further and further away from expressing your unique value.

Personally, I only use time-based pricing for those tasks where time is all I offer. For example, I might quote a daily rate for visiting a client's site, or attending an event that they're organizing. For these activities, there isn't really any value or output beyond the event itself, so it's appropriate to charge for the time it takes. (If I *do* have to produce an output as well as attending, that's charged separately.)

One sign that time-based pricing isn't working for you is when you put together your final invoice for a job, and it just looks way too low. Although it accurately records the time you've put into the project, it's not a fair reflection of the value the client is getting out. That demoralizes you, and might even make you resent the client themselves – even though they're only paying what you asked for.

This discrepancy between value and time will probably become more pronounced as you advance through your freelance career. After a few years, you find that you can now do some jobs a lot more quickly, but with no compromise on quality. Indeed, there might be some things you can do both quicker *and* better, because you know so much more about what does and doesn't work. If you stick with time-based pricing, you'll end up receiving lower pay for superior work – which obviously isn't the best route to your financial goals.

Of course, this argument assumes that you are honest about the time you've put in. A hazard with time-based pricing is that you wind up massaging the hours column so the invoice total is a fairer reflection of value.

It's fine to set a minimum charge (say, half a day) to avoid tiny invoices that aren't worth the trouble of issuing. But if you're regularly inflating hours spent, that's simply dishonest – and might even be regarded as fraud. Also, you'll have to make sure you maintain the deception in a consistent way, so you never get caught out. Overall, honesty is the best policy.

You could try to compensate for these problems by simply jacking up your hourly rate. But you might still run into problems with consistency. For example, your high hourly rate might work really well for short, high-value jobs, but result in astronomical totals for longer but more mundane tasks.

To compensate for this, you might consider applying a discount to your own quote, or setting different rates for different jobs. But really, all you're doing is rejigging your rates to reverse-engineer the price you want to charge. These are all clear signals that you should really be charging by the project. So go with the flow and do it.

A similar point applies to quantity-based rates, such as charging for copywriting by the word. I once tried to set up a per-word pricing structure that would reflect my unique value, but I soon got into a hideous mess. Since every project was different, I found that I was constantly making exceptions to my own rules, or submitting invoices that even *I* didn't really believe were a fair reflection of the value I'd delivered. After a few weeks – and some *very* awkward conversations with clients – I gave up on the idea for good.

Having said all that, time-based pricing does have its place. For some types of work, such as enterprise-grade software development, it's extremely difficult – if not impossible – to gauge the time required for a project in advance. There are simply too many unknowns, too many factors at play and too many insights that only emerge once you're well into the work. In this situation, an hourly rate protects both you and your client against uncertainty – but it also means you can no longer offer the reassurance of a price that's fixed up front.

14 Consider every factor

So, what areas should you take into account when setting your project prices? Here are the main things you'll want to consider:

- *Your unique value*: all the benefits that the client gets from your service, both tangible and intangible
- *Your skills and experience*: who you've worked for, doing which tasks and for how long – and how your abilities relate to this project
- *Your brand and reputation* in the market, which determine how prospects perceive your service at the time they get in touch
- The nature of the *market* for your service, and what people tend to charge (although there's probably a wide range)
- *Your location*, which can affect your cost of living and people's perceptions of costs
- *The prospect's location*, which might affect their own revenues or their willingness to pay top dollar

- If your prospect is a company, the *nature of their business* and the *size and age of their company*, all of which might affect their resources and cash flow.

These factors differ by nature. Let's break them down and take a closer look.

The ones near the top of the list are attributes of yourself or your service. While it's within your power to develop them, you can't change them instantly at the point when a prospect gets in touch. So you can only respond on the basis of who you are and what you offer right now.

For example, your skills and experience evolve only gradually. Therefore, it's just a question of how relevant they are to the project at hand, and how much value they offer to the client. If your skills are specialized, you may be able to charge more (as we'll see in chapter 7).

The rest of the market is something you should take into account, but without letting it define you. As we've seen, the value you offer is unique, so you don't necessarily have to charge what other people charge. However, you may need to think about how your price looks in context, and consider the best way to frame it (as we'll see in chapter 4).

Other factors are specific to the client. This implies that you might charge different prices for different clients – even if you're doing exactly the same work for both. And this is an area where your own preferences come into play.

Some freelancers feel they should have consistent prices for everyone, and not chop and change or offer different prices in parallel. This may be because they feel it's dishonest, or at least untransparent, to take a 'horses for courses' approach.

For example, in the world of travel and leisure, Airbnb's 'smart pricing' can automatically optimize the price for a particular stay in response to demand, with the aim of maximizing bookings for the host. But that can cause irritation and confusion for the user, who can't understand why the prices they see online are fluctuating over time. You might feel that by tailoring the price to the client, you're playing a similar trick – even if no individual client ever actually discovers what you've done.

However, for other freelancers, it goes without saying that different clients have different price expectations, and that they should cut their coat according to the client's cloth. The most obvious example is charities, who are likely to have fewer resources than large, profitable firms. But some freelancers also scale back their prices for smaller firms, and charge bigger firms more, purely on the basis of their respective ability or willingness to pay.

Personally, I tend towards the variable-price approach. The main reason is I think it makes sense to charge new clients more, rather than operating a fixed tariff that you increase for everyone across the board.

I also want the option to vary my prices in response to demand. Not so much lowering the rate to win the work during lean times, but more to increase it when I'm busy. If you're already booked up and a new enquiry comes in, it makes sense to quote high, in the hope that you will ultimately be able to swap a lower-paying client for a new, higher-paying one.

We'll dive deep into this theme in chapter 6, when we look at ways to increase your prices.

15 Set profitable precedents

For freelancers, repeat business is gold.

You know and trust the client. You understand their business. You know how they like to work, and what they expect from you. You know that they're happy with your work, and what it costs. And last but not least, you know that they will actually pay your invoice.

New-business approaches are great, and you obviously need them in order to grow your business. But they're still an unknown quantity, and bringing a new client on board will always take more effort than serving an existing one. Therefore, acquiring new business imposes a time overhead that reduces the time you can spend on fee-earning work. The foundation of a profitable freelance business is a set of reliable repeat clients who keep coming back.

That's why it's vital to set profitable precedents, by doing deals that you're prepared to repeat. Whatever price you offer to a new prospect, you should set it at a level that you'll still be happy with if they come back for five or 10 similar jobs in the future. Once you've agreed that price, you'll be able to refer back to it in future price negotiations – for example, by saying 'This price is in line with what I charged for project X last year.'

It's easy to think you *have* to quote low for the first job, in order to safely land the client. But you're simply storing up difficulty and frustration for later on, when you realize that you either have to keep on pricing at the same level, or open an awkward conversation about increasing prices.

You may tell yourself that this rate is strictly an introductory offer, and that you'll increase the price on the very next job. But a more likely outcome is that you wind up waiting a year or so before you feel able to ask for more, kicking yourself the whole time.

Even if the client actually asks you for an introductory discount, try to hold firm. You should only offer discounts on confirmed quantities of work, not promises. We'll come back to this in chapter 5, when we dive deep into negotiation.

16 Charge for everything

The rest of this chapter looks at things you can include in your price. And its guiding principle is *charge for everything*.

Every activity that adds value for the client, or advances the project, should be included in your quote. That includes the physical, hands-on tasks that result in tangible 'deliverables', but also those tasks that don't generate any solid output – like carrying out research, taking part in discussions or just thinking up ideas. You should also include supporting tasks, such as project management, if they are going to represent a significant part of the project.

You don't necessarily have to break out all these elements and itemize them as separate costs in your proposal, but the overall fee for the project should always reflect them. (We'll come back to presenting your prices in the next chapter.)

One crucial point here is that everything you charge for should be genuine. I'm not suggesting that you try to cram *everything* mentioned below into every proposal, or that you artificially inflate your proposal with fake tasks. This isn't about deception or sharp practice. It's about recognizing all the types of value that you offer and being fairly rewarded for them.

Also, this list isn't necessarily exhaustive. If there's another element relevant to your work that I haven't mentioned here, by all means include it.

17 Charge for meetings

Meetings aren't just 'talking about' the project. They're an integral part of the work itself. The input you provide during a meeting can form a significant part of the value you deliver – potentially even the biggest.

For example, in an initial briefing meeting, you might propose ideas that have a decisive influence on how the rest of the project unfolds. You might shut down an ill-advised option that would have cost the client a lot of time or money, had they gone ahead with it. Or you might offer advice that will add value for the client even if the rest of the project doesn't go ahead.

That's why I think you should always charge for a meeting, if it's required as part of the project.

Now, you might feel that there are some meetings that really shouldn't be chargeable. For example, if your dream client gets in touch and requests an exploratory chat, you might not want to put *anything* in the way of that happening. That's fine, but bear in mind you could be setting a precedent that you might need to revisit later on – and the prospect clearly likes meeting up, so this could turn into a regular thing.

If my established clients ask to meet me about a project, I normally just mention up front that it will be chargeable – usually at half a day, once travelling time is taken into account. At the meeting, I learn about the project, which enables me to quote for the work. I then roll the cost for the meeting into my quote for the whole thing. So my project price includes the work I'm about to do, plus the meeting I've already attended. If this price is then declined, in theory I can invoice for the meeting alone – but in practice, it very rarely happens.

Some freelancers do believe you should offer meetings for free – at least for new prospects. The idea is you throw your bread on the waters and it comes back to you tenfold. But I feel this approach turns a meeting that should be a collaboration into an interview, a sales pitch or a game. You should be focusing on what's right for the project, but instead, you're scheming to win the business – while possibly also trying to minimize your commitment in terms of time and expertise. As a result, you're probably not helping the client – or yourself.

If you accept that meetings have value to the client, then attending them for free is not that different from offering a free sample (see chapter 5). It may *feel* physically less demanding, because you can just sit there and chat, instead of doing hands-on work. But there could still be huge value in the ideas and feedback you're sharing with the client.

These days, meetings are increasingly likely to be held online. While that might drastically reduce the time required to take part, it doesn't necessarily reduce the value you'll contribute. So on the principle of charging for anything that adds value, online meetings and client interviews should still be included in your price.

With virtual meetings, you may also have to guard against being pulled into a meeting ad hoc. While a client can't really call you into their office at five minutes' notice, they *might* get away with tapping you up for a quick Skype chat, which then turns into something more time-consuming. Learn to spot the signs – and set your status to 'offline' if you need to.

18 Charge for site visits

When I say 'site visit', I mean any activity where you go to the client's premises to talk to the other people involved in a project or gather information to support your work.

For example, as a copywriter, I might talk to the people who've developed a product that I will be helping to promote, or call-centre staff who talk to the client's own customers every day. This gets me closer to the 'voice of the customer' that is such a vital part of engaging copy.

Site visits are enormously valuable. You'll learn loads about the client's organization, their team and their working culture.

And precisely because you learn so much, so quickly, it can be tempting to throw them in for free. After all, it'll help you do the work, plus it'll be a fun day out – right?

Right. But here's the thing: *what helps you helps the client too*. All that stuff you're learning isn't for your own entertainment. It will make the client's project go better. And that's why your learning time should not be given away for free.

19 Charge for research

Like site visits, desk research can be an important part of a project. For example, you might need to spend time getting up to speed with the client's industry, the types of customers they serve or their competitors. Or you might need to research a market before you can suggest a product or service to suit your client.

You might be tempted to roll research into your hands-on work, perhaps without mentioning it to the client at all. Don't. This is an important part of a project, not a minor subsidiary task that you 'just do' so you can get started on the 'real work'. And you certainly shouldn't be rushing it because you realized, too late, that you should have included it in your price but didn't. To guard against that, consider early on whether reading or research will be required, and make sure it features in your proposal.

Sometimes, clients will dump a load of reading material on you after you've agreed the price, in which case you should ideally go back and revise it, if you feel you can. However, be sure that the material is actually relevant, and not just 'FYI' stuff that you probably don't need to look at anyway.

20 Charge for thinking

Your client isn't just hiring a pair of hands. They're hiring a mind – yours.

All things are created twice: first mentally, in the mind of the creator, and then physically, in the material world. And your client should pay for both these steps.

To illustrate this, let's take an extreme example. How long would it take to 'write' Nike's slogan, 'Just Do It'?

If by 'writing' you mean simply typing the words out, the answer is 2.5 seconds. You could go to a content mill charging 1.5p a word and get change from 5p.

But of course, what we call 'writing' is not just physically tapping on a keyboard, or manipulating a pen. It is *thinking* about what to say, and how to say it.

The same point applies to your freelance work. It's not just about the time you spend with mouse, trowel or kitchen knife in hand – whatever the tools of your trade may be. It's also about the time you spend making sure your hands-on work will actually deliver value.

When you look at it this way, it's clear that the thinking is actually way more important than the doing. Without thinking, there can be no doing. If there's not enough thinking, or the thinking is wrong, no amount of doing will achieve the aim. The first, mental creation *determines* the second, physical one.

That's why the client really doesn't actually want you to just dive in and start doing or making stuff – however anxious they may be for results or quick delivery. So you may need to explain to them that it will take longer than they thought to make the journey from brief to final output.

For writers like me, the thinking phase is when we make sense of the stuff we learned from our research. We need to 'chew it over' and consider how to make new connections between all the disparate bits of knowledge we've taken on board. This process takes time and it can't really be rushed. I'm sure freelancers in many other areas experience something very similar.

Quite often, the mental 'digestion' happens away from the desk. Ideas suddenly pop up during a shower, a dog walk or even a nap. But even though this takes place in what is officially 'downtime', it still helps the client. In fact, you could argue that this 'background processing' is more valuable than anything else you do. You're turning over your *whole mind*, both conscious and unconscious, to the client's project, allowing their work to invade your inner life and displace your most intimate thoughts.

I've grown accustomed to this, and I don't have a problem immersing myself in a client's project. But equally, their work is not allowed to live rent-free in my head. Brainpower costs.

How should you describe the thinking phase? I usually call it 'developing ideas', but the answer will depend on the nature of your own work. If you're worried that it just sounds too insubstantial, you could combine it with research, which sounds more solid and hands-on – although it underplays the element of creation.

Alternatively, you might manifest the mental side of your work as a higher rate for hands-on tasks, reflecting the level of commitment you will bring to them. For example, the rate I charge for academic editing is higher than the market average – but I feel it's justified, because I spend a great deal of time reflecting on my work, often rethinking and revising my edits and comments several times before I'm done. I don't put 'thinking' on the invoice, but the overall rate reflects it nonetheless.

21 Charge for writing supporting notes

Depending on what type of work you do, writing supporting notes can be a vital part of the value you add.

Supporting notes make intangible value visible, by capturing the results of the thinking phase (see above). You then combine them with your hands-on work to form an integrated whole that shows the client the results from both the tangible and intangible sides of your work. In other words, they can see both the thinking *and* the doing.

Supporting notes aren't intended to show the client how much work you've done (although they may have that effect). Instead, they're about making an explicit case for your decisions, so the client doesn't have to infer it. With notes, your ideas don't have to stand alone.

For example, when I'm asked to create product names or taglines, the actual content I produce might come to fewer than 50 words. However, as a deliverable to be sent to the client, that handful of words doesn't come close to telling the full story. So I tell it.

Along with my work, I'll also provide a full, detailed rationale that helps my client understand my work and the thinking behind it. For example, if I'm proposing product names, I'll explain where each one is derived from, the tone or feeling it evokes, its advantages and its drawbacks. I'll also point out the inevitable trade-offs between all these things, and add any other thoughts I feel are relevant.

Without these notes, my ideas on their own would be hopelessly puny. I'd probably have to schedule a call to discuss them – but by then, my client might have already formed a view. Supporting notes help to manage expectations when the client sees your work for the first time, because they are right there alongside it.

The interesting thing about supporting notes – the dangerous thing, some might say – is that they let the client go 'behind the curtain' and enter your working process. Instead of presenting your one best solution in a finished state, like a fired pot, you let the client wander into your studio and watch you shape the clay. Once there, they can pick up half-formed or second-rate ideas and potentially combine them in new and less desirable ways. So when you're writing your notes, consider carefully whether you really want to reveal *all* your thoughts – even in a document that ostensibly presents 'your thinking' on a problem. Overall, though, I feel these downsides are outweighed by the sense of trust and collaboration that's created.

Another potential pitfall of supporting notes is that they put you in the position of critiquing your own work. If you're talking pros and cons, you may need to explain to your client that every choice involves compromise, and that there will never be a solution that's all pros with no cons.

On your side, remember that it is fiendishly difficult to form an objective opinion on your own work in isolation. So when explaining downsides, you may need to temper your self-doubt. You don't want to talk the client out of an idea before they've even properly considered it – or reject an idea yourself that the client might actually have loved. It might help to sleep on it and re-read your notes the next morning to make sure they're fair. Time always reveals the true value of ideas.

22   Charge for managing the project

Once you go freelance, you realize how much of your time is spent on non-productive admin tasks like drafting emails, preparing prices, doing your accounts and chasing invoices. You can easily get through to lunchtime without doing a stroke of 'real work'. So if you'll be coordinating a project for a client – or just certain aspects of it – you need to make sure you get paid.

It's easy to neglect project management because, although you're really a small business, you still give yourself a 'job title' that reflects your hands-on work. You then start thinking of yourself as (say) 'a web designer'. In your mind, you draw a boundary around the tasks that make up 'your job' and exclude everything else. That puts up a psychological barrier against charging for other stuff, because you think of it as out of scope, or above your paygrade.

Maybe you don't particularly want to manage projects, preferring to focus on your core tasks. I don't blame you – but on some jobs, it's inevitable. Sometimes, you can get drawn into it by default, simply because other people don't step up.

For example, say you're designing a website, and the client asks you to liaise with their chosen photographer to obtain the imagery you need. But it turns out that they're always out on assignments, so you have to spend hours chasing them up, even though you have no real authority over them.

You know this situation is wrong, but you still hesitate to blow the whistle, because you want to seem easy-going and amenable. All the hassle takes time that you could be spending on other things – and also drains your enthusiasm, because you're not getting paid to run the show.

As this illustration shows, you need to anticipate project-management tasks in order to charge for them. Otherwise, you'll have to go back and ask the client for payment after the fact, which is tricky. So if you know other people will be involved in the project, you'll need to clarify at the briefing stage whether and how you'll be working with them, or if the client will take care of everything on your behalf.

Project management can include:

- Liaising with everyone involved in the project
- Interviews to gather information

- Setting up and leading meetings
- Creating written plans and schedules, and making sure people stick to them
- Getting prices and monitoring costs
- Dealing with suppliers, including briefing them, preparing material for them or checking their work
- Reporting back to the client on progress
- Commissioning other freelancers and overseeing their work.

Reading through that list, you might be thinking that it sounds like a nightmare. There's no doubt that managing a project could push you beyond your existing skillset. However, the upside is that taking on these things can make you indispensable to the client: a 'safe pair of hands' to whom they can entrust important projects and be sure that they'll get done. And reliable project managers don't come cheap.

23 Charge for changes

It's rare to get a whole project completely right first time, and the larger and more complex the project, the less likely it becomes. So you'll want to include some scope in your price for handling changes requested by the client.

Most clients are perfectly reasonable about the level of changes they ask for. But some may ask for change after change, to the point where you spend longer 'amending' the work than you did creating it in the first place. At the extreme, the project goes into a death-spiral, as you lose sight of the goal completely and descend into a hopeless, endless quest for a holy grail that might not even exist.

Thankfully, such problems are rare. And you can nip them in the bud by making sure the brief and agreement are watertight before you start. However, you do need to agree what level of changes will be included in the normal course of the project.

The simplest approach is to build changes into your project price. For example, I tell clients that my price includes two rounds of modest changes based on their feedback. My rationale here is that if we still haven't got it right after two rounds, we either need to revisit the brief, or agree that I can't help them and go our separate ways.

But what does 'modest' mean? Well, if clients consult my terms and conditions, they'll discover that I define it as 'affecting less than 10% of the work'. So, in theory, if I end up changing 20% of the words I've written, I can go back to them and seek to agree an additional charge.

My terms use an objective measure – word count – to define the threshold of acceptable changes. If you don't have a measure like that, you might have to use a time measure instead (for instance, changes that take longer than X hours to carry out will be charged extra).

In practice, though, I've rarely had to use this fall-back option. Simply by having it in place and stating it up front, you flag up to your clients that there's a limit to what you will do. Most will respect it.

Incidentally, I have seen a couple of freelancers doing the exact opposite of what I suggest here. On their sites, they say something like 'We'll keep working until you're satisfied.' I can see the appeal of this as a market differentiator, but at the level of project management, it seems like a magnet for timewasters. Your prospects might infer that you'll *never* get it right first time – or even that you won't even try to, and simply rely on multiple iterations of feedback from them to get you over the line. So, speaking personally, I don't recommend this approach.

24 Charge for extras

In project management, 'scope creep' is the tendency for new requirements to be added to a project in an uncontrolled way, so the scope gradually expands way beyond the original vision. It's sometimes called 'kitchen sink syndrome', because you wind up including 'everything and the kitchen sink'.

Scope creep can be a problem for freelancers too. If you're not careful, you can get drawn into spending far more time on a project than you anticipated, for no additional reward. So it's up to you, as the *de facto* project manager, to recognize scope creep when it happens, and decide whether or not to charge for the extra work.

Because scope creep is gradual by its nature, it can creep up on you without you realizing. You're working away on the client's suggested changes when you think, 'Wait a minute. We never agreed to this!' So to help you spot it, let's look at some of the ways it can happen.

Sometimes, scope creep is the natural result of emerging insight: the understanding that only comes from actually getting deep in the weeds of a complex project. As long as you have a written record of the original brief, it should be straightforward to establish that neither you nor the client anticipated this requirement, and therefore it will cost extra.

At the other end of the scale, scope creep can also arise from honest misunderstandings about what is and isn't included, even on the simplest projects. For example, when I work for clients who are new to marketing, they sometimes assume that I'll design their leaflet as well as write it. So I have to explain that what they think of as simply 'doing a leaflet' actually involves more tasks and skills than they thought.

Here, the key is to make it crystal clear upfront what you are offering to do. Don't be afraid of excluding things you may feel are obvious, just to avoid all doubt.

At other times, scope creep is the result of what I call *inflation of expectation*. It definitely happens with copywriting, and it probably happens with other types of work too.

Say you're working on a project, and the client likes what you've done. So far, so good. But then, as the project unfolds, the client starts to take the results you've already achieved for granted. From their insider's viewpoint, they can no longer imagine how the project would look to someone seeing it for the first time.

Having lost perspective, the client gets anxious that what you've done so far won't be enough. So they heap more and more demands on the project, trying to add more content or features to something that's fine as it is. This just dilutes the impact of the project, and there's a real danger that you won't even achieve the essential aims you agreed at the outset.

If you feel the work is spilling out beyond its boundaries, you may need to politely remind the client of what this project is supposed to be about. It may also help to get an outside perspective – for example, through user testing, or just a second opinion. Or you might be able to suggest splitting the project into two or more parts, each focused on a single aim.

Finally, you have to consider the possibility that the client who asks for extras is actually trying to get some work for free, while feigning innocence. If you suspect this is the case, it's not really worth trying to accommodate them. Just state bluntly that what they're asking for is an extra, and it will cost. And regardless of what comes out of that, make absolutely sure you get paid for what was originally agreed.

25 Point out extras without charging

Once you've noticed scope creep, you have to decide whether to raise it with the client and ask for more money. Depending on your client's personality, you might feel apprehensive about doing that. They might react by accusing you of being nit-picky or 'difficult to work with'. Or they might not agree that their request constitutes an extra at all.

If the new requirement is small in relation to the whole project, you might be tempted to keep quiet and throw it in for free. But if you do that, you risk setting an unwelcome precedent – whether for this project, or future ones. You have to draw the line somewhere. So if the line isn't here, where is it? Or are you just ducking the issue for fear of rocking the boat?

If you're worried about these issues, remember that you're only pointing out what has been agreed – and being completely professional about it too. But there's also a third, less confrontational way to go. You could point out to the client that they're asking for extra stuff, but without actually charging for it. So you say something like, 'This is beyond the original scope of the project, but I'm happy to keep the price at the level we agreed.'

This signals two things to the client: first, this is an extra; and second, you would normally charge for it. That puts down a marker that will make it easier to charge this client for extras on future projects – or just discourage them from requesting them in the first place. If you help the client stay within a fixed budget that they can't control, they may feel they owe you a favour, and look more kindly on higher prices in the future.

The wider context of the deal makes a difference. For example, say I've edited 10,000 words for a client and invoiced for it, and they then ask me to edit another 50 words they just inserted. Here, the scope of the project hasn't really changed, and the only value I'm offering is convenience. So I don't make a fuss or raise another invoice; I just do the extra bit and say, 'There's no charge for this.' In this situation, I'd rather have the goodwill that comes from making life easy for the client than squeeze an extra drop of cash out of them.

26 Charge for 'just having a look'

Sometimes, clients will ask you to 'just have a look' at something, on the basis that because it won't take you very long, or you won't have to 'do' very much, you shouldn't be charging for it. They may make this argument explicitly, or they may leave it unsaid.

However, as we've seen, you charge for *value*, not time or effort. And for some of these jobs, a little of your time or effort might go a very long way.

For example, imagine you're asking a lawyer to look over a five-page contract that a client has given you to carry out a colossal, five-figure freelance job. It might only take them 30 minutes to review it, at the end of which they say, 'Yes, everything's fine.' They then hand you a bill for £200 – which you gladly pay.

In a narrow, physical sense, they've hardly *done* anything at all. They 'just had a look'. However, their 'just looking' still delivered huge value for you. Before, you had no understanding or control – but now you have knowledge, security and the freedom to proceed with your deal. So while nothing tangible has really happened, the intangible benefit you get is immense.

The lesson here is that your knowledge and experience can deliver huge value for clients, even when you don't really 'do' that much. It's the time and effort you put in over the years *before* the job that allows you to create value in the here-and-now. And that value only comes at a price.

However, not every little job necessarily carries so much value. So when you get a request like this, you have to consider what the client gets out of the deal, and whether you feel OK just throwing it in for no charge.

27 Charge for late payment

I can't believe any freelancer really enjoys chasing for payment. You've done the work and put in your invoice; in your mind, the job is done and dusted. Then the client stalls on payment, forcing you to chase them up. So you waste time that you could be spending on fee-paying work – and your confidence takes a hit too.

Charging for late payment helps in one of two ways. First and foremost, it gives the client an incentive to pay sooner, and as a secondary benefit, you can charge them extra if they don't. It's really the first of these outcomes that you're aiming for. In other words, what you want is prompt payment, rather than to generate bonus revenue from late payers. OK, you get to add on the late-payment charge – but they still haven't actually paid, and you don't get a penny until they do. So you *still* have to spend time chasing for payment, and the small extra reward won't really compensate you for that time. (To give your client an extra incentive to pay up, you could offer a discount for prompt payment – say, 5% off if they pay within seven days.)

To charge for late payment, make sure your invoice clearly states your payment terms. Most freelancers allow 30 days, but some opt for two weeks or even 'due on receipt'. Then, add a note to the invoice stating that you'll charge a certain percentage of the invoice value for each month the invoice goes unpaid – a typical value is 1.5% per month. You'll also want to include this in any contract you agree with clients. Make sure you check the regulations in your country to find out what you can charge.[3]

If your invoice goes unpaid, submit a new one showing the interest and/or late-payment fees, so the client can see the amount steadily increasing. That should encourage them to pay up, and hopefully pay more quickly in future.

Consistently late-paying clients are a real headache. I've had some clients who, while they always paid in the end, also seemed to have a company-wide policy of 'Don't pay until they chase.' (Maybe I'm paranoid, but it could even have been 'Don't pay *freelancers* until they chase.') On an emotional level, it's demoralizing when people make you jump through hoops like this. But on a practical level, it's actually not too difficult to deal with, once you understand the rules of the game.

Other delays are just down to problems with internal administration. Your own contact wants you to be paid, and is embarrassed by the delay, but they still can't get their accounts department to play ball. So you have to set your own limits on how much delay is acceptable, and decide on a case-by-case basis whether late payment is a danger sign or just another overhead.

When you're chasing for payment, stay completely in your money mind, not your work mind. This is not like working on a project, or even negotiating a price, where you need a bit of give and take to oil the wheels. So don't get side-tracked by worries about upsetting the client. You've fulfilled your side of the

---

[3] In the UK, freelancers are allowed by law to charge interest at 8% over the Bank of England base rate, plus fixed penalty fees if the debt isn't paid within 30 days. The fees are £40 for debts under £1000, £70 for up to £10,000 and £100 beyond that point. Since these fees apply to each individual invoice, it makes sense to invoice for each piece of work separately, instead of including multiple jobs on a single invoice.

bargain, and now it's time for the client to fulfil theirs. No decent client will get crabby about you chasing for money that's rightfully due.

When two people make a deal, both sides must honour their commitments. So if you really struggle with this, just imagine the opposite scenario. Your client paid in advance... but then you didn't do the work! That's right – you just sat on your ass, sipping a cappuccino and scrolling through Facebook. Do you really think your client would hesitate for *one second* to email and tell you to get going? Exactly.

Takeaways from this chapter

- Pricing by the project is nearly always the best way to reflect your unique value and maximize your earnings.

- Make sure you consider every factor that could influence the prices you set.

- Precedents are powerful, so get them working for you and not against you.

- Charge for every task or activity, whether physical or mental, that adds value for your client, plus extra work and late payment.

4 PRESENTING YOUR PRICES

Image is everything, particularly when it comes to price. In this chapter, we'll look at how to present your prices so they appear diligent, professional and fair.

28 Frame every price

On the face of it, giving someone a price seems like a simple, fairly transactional process. The prospect tells you what they need, and you tell them what it will cost. Then, the prospect goes off and makes a buying decision – a process that you have no knowledge of, or control over.

That's true as far as it goes. But it misses out the golden opportunity you have to communicate with the prospect during the pricing process – partly by telling, and partly by showing.

At a literal level, you *tell* them what you'll do, and what you'd like to charge for it. But at a meta level, you *show* them how much care you take over your work, how much knowledge you're bringing to this project and how important the prospect's work is to you. By covering both these bases, you give yourself the best chance of winning the work.

To see why this is so, consider what happens if you do the opposite. If you give prospects a price as a simple number, they have no frame of reference for it at all. If you're up against other providers, the prospect won't appreciate the unique value you offer, which those other guys can't provide. So you look 'expensive' by default, even though you might actually offer more value – and better value for money, when everything is taken into account.

That's why it's so important to frame every price in the right way, so prospects understand and interpret it the way *you* want.

29 Ask relevant questions, if you can

Prospects may not have their brief fully nailed down at the time they get in touch. Instead, they'll have a fairly clear idea of the final outcome they want, but only a hazy sense of the elements that will go into it, or the process through which it will be reached.

For example, my prospects will frequently ask about my cost to write a website. Obviously, they've seen plenty of websites before, and they know what a website is. But if they haven't decided how many pages theirs will have, requesting a price is like asking, 'How long is a piece of string?'

Others might have gone further by developing a site map (a diagram of all the pages in the site and how they link together). But they still haven't decided how long each page will be, or how it will look.

Then there are those who've approached the problem from a different angle. They've created wireframes (rough page designs), or even coded a few actual pages. But they've only worked on the most high-profile parts of the site, then tailed off without considering how the rest of it will work.

Don't get me wrong – I'm not criticizing these prospects. A project like a website is tough to scope out all on your own, particularly when you're not an expert. And helping with the planning is an important part of my job.

Besides, I don't see this lack of clarity as a problem. In fact, I welcome it – because it's a chance for me to help the prospect, while also showcasing my own knowledge. As I guide the prospect forward, I can show them that I know what I'm talking about, by asking informed and pointed questions to clear up the grey areas.

As you consider a project, the three main areas you need to cover are:

- What is the target outcome?
- How much work is involved?
- What will the working process be?

Once you have answers to these questions, you'll be able to build up a price according to the elements we saw in chapter 3.

How you ask your questions is up to you. Since I'm a natural introvert, I prefer writing, where I can decide exactly what I want to say and take as long as I want over the reply. However, if you're more outgoing, you might welcome the chance to call your prospect and have a friendly chat.

Even if your question is only minor – for example, clarifying a particular aspect of the working process – it's still worth asking it. By picking up on this one little thing, you show that you are alert to *all* the details of the project, just as a good lawyer will pounce on the loopholes in a contract.

Again, you can see the value of this approach by considering the opposite. When I was starting out, I would sometimes submit my price without taking the time to fully understand the project. With the arrogance of youth, I imagined that I could just intuit what the prospect wanted – or failing that, that everything would sort itself out later on. I was probably also a bit shy of 'making a fuss', as I saw it, and anxious to reel the client in and start work.

That was a mistake, and it taught me two important lessons. First, freelancers aren't mind-readers, and trying to second-guess a project spec is a fool's game. Second, if you start a project and *then* realize that your quote was too low, you face a choice between eating the extra work or attempting to renegotiate the price, which is guaranteed to irritate your client. Needless to say, neither of these options is a fast-track to riches.

However, there are some caveats. I think it's possible to ask *too many* questions at this stage. You should certainly ask enough questions to clarify the brief, but continuing beyond that point brings no further benefit. Don't ask questions that are only intended to show off your knowledge, or those that the prospect clearly can't answer at this stage.

If you over-interrogate the prospect, they may start wondering why they have to do so much explaining, when *you're* supposed to be the expert. They might ask themselves if you actually know what you're doing. Or they might even feel that you're trying to shift your own responsibility for the project on to their shoulders – covering your own ass so that if the project goes wrong, you can say you were just doing what you were told.

Also, remember that questions are always a hold-up. However good your intentions may be, you're still putting hurdles in the way of a deal, which gives the prospect an opportunity to choose another path of less resistance. So keep your questions focused on the essential knowledge you need to quote – not nice-to-know stuff that can wait until later. As we saw in chapter 3, you can address more detailed research as part of the project itself – for example, in a kick-off call before you start the work.

30 Write a detailed proposal

Once you've clarified the brief and established what you're going to charge for, you can bring it all together in a proposal that you pass over to the prospect – most likely by email.

For larger jobs in particular, your proposal needs to have some detail. Quoting a simple price with no accompanying narrative looks passive, complacent and lazy. On a practical level, you're leaving it to the prospect to quiz you about your approach – or, worse, just make their own assumptions. And on a relationship level, you're telling them that you don't really care that much about their work.

So instead, put some meat on the bones by covering some or all of these areas:

- The *tasks* you'll carry out (probably itemized as bullet points)
- What the final *output* will be, and how it will be delivered (for example, a personalized fitness plan, provided as a PDF and a printed copy)
- The *working process* that you will follow, including anything the prospect will have to do in support (for example, provide more information, approve your work and so on)
- For clarity, *tasks that you won't do*, or things that you *won't* deliver (for example, you *will* write the copy for a website, but you *won't* upload it to WordPress). Experience will teach you which tasks clients tend to assume are included
- Other *relevant work* you've done in the past, with contact info for referees if appropriate
- How much it will *cost*, including any relevant sales tax (such as VAT in the UK)

- Terms and practical details for *payment* – when you'll invoice (including any partial or upfront payments), when payment will be due, whether you prefer bank transfer or PayPal, and so on

- Any important *milestones* within the project (for example, rough sketches, designs, finished artwork), with timings and part-payments due if appropriate

- When you can *start* (which might be conditional on the project being confirmed by a certain time – for example, 'If you give me the go-ahead today, I can start this week')

- *How long* the project will take overall – either a hard deadline on a specific date, or a relative 'floating timescale' if your schedule depends on other timings

- Any other relevant *terms and conditions* (or you could just link to them, if they're available online).

Creating a detailed proposal is a great way to convey important information to your prospect, and to show them the many facets of the value you provide. But it sends important meta-messages too. It shows that you've been around long enough to develop a working method, which in turn implies that you'll know how to avoid common pitfalls. It shows that you've got enough experience to anticipate likely questions. And it shows that you're proactive and thoughtful enough to create the proposal in the first place.

If you're like me, your initial interaction with the client is probably taking place over email, so that's the natural place to provide your proposal. However, a longer proposal might be too unwieldy in that format – so consider creating a nicely styled PDF instead. It looks more professional and, for more significant projects, makes it easier for the client to share your proposal around internally, with no risk of anything getting accidentally missed off or deleted. You can also include things like terms and conditions, which might make an email too long and cumbersome.

31 Itemize costs as well as tasks

I've suggested itemizing all the tasks involved in a project. But should you also give itemized *prices* for each element – like on a restaurant bill? Or is it better just to list the various tasks, and quote an overall project fee that covers them all?

At the end of the day, it's your call. By itemizing prices, you make it crystal clear that each task takes time and has value. You might also feel that the total price looks more reasonable when the prospect can see what 'building blocks' go into it. (We've all done a double-take at a restaurant bill, before the breakdown reminds us about the three beers and extra fries we conveniently forgot.)

On the downside, you might be giving the prospect too much information by itemizing prices. You might encourage them to start questioning why this or that task costs so much, or to pick and choose items from the 'menu' in the hope of reducing the price.

To address this, you'll want to decide in advance whether you'll allow that sort of customization, and if so, whether the project will still stack up for you once certain elements have been taken out. Some customized configurations may work, while others won't. And if you do allow the client to omit anything, you'll want to explain the implications of their choice.

For example, say you're a personal trainer and you need to introduce a new client to the gym. You probably won't allow them to skip their induction session and get straight to training, for reasons of safety. So even though that element might be itemized, it's still a compulsory part of the project.

32 Develop proposal modules and information sheets

As you've probably realized, writing a detailed proposal takes some work. So you'll want to weigh the value of the project, the profile of the prospect and the likelihood of future work against the time and effort you put into creating the proposal. That means doing a quick mental calculation of the potential lifetime value of the prospect – as difficult as that may be.

One way to cut down the grunt-work of creating proposals is to develop a set of reusable content modules that you can use to quickly knock up a proposal tailored to a prospect. For instance, you might find you often wind up saying something similar about what is included and excluded from the project, so you can create a standardized text for that part.

Alternatively, you could create a generic information sheet that can be reused exactly as it is for multiple prospects. Over the years, I noticed that new clients for my academic editing tended to ask the same sorts of questions. So I wrote a detailed document explaining exactly what I do. Now, when new prospects get in touch, I can simply send them the document and it sells the service on my behalf.

Again, there's a double purpose here: I convey the information in a way that's hassle-free for both sides, but I also demonstrate that I'm serious about my work.

33 Charge for proposals

Since writing a detailed proposal is labour-intensive, you might even want to charge for it, in some cases. With the client's agreement, you separate off the task of developing the proposal and make it a chargeable project in itself.

This approach swaps one set of risks for another. On the upside, you can safely put a lot of time into the proposal, since you're now being compensated for it. And you will get at least some reward if the client takes your proposal and hands it to someone else to put into practice. That scenario is unlikely, but it could happen.

On the downside, you also create a natural break-point at the time when you submit your proposal and invoice for your work so far. When that point comes, the client can decide to reject your proposal or just sit on it indefinitely – waiting for the right time to invest, perhaps. If that happens, it will be up to you to chase the client up and kick-start the project again.

Takeaways from this chapter

- Always give your price context. Numbers on their own are not persuasive.

- If you can ask relevant questions, do so. They're a chance to position yourself as an expert.

- Write detailed proposals for larger jobs. Use text modules to make it quicker and easier.

- For very large jobs, consider charging for your proposal.

5 NEGOTIATING DEALS

You want to agree a good price, but you don't want to get caught up in a tug of war over price alone. So be like a professional negotiator, and reach a deal by bringing in factors that offer value to both sides.

34 Stay frosty

Negotiating on price is a test for both your head and your heart. It takes technical skill, but it also requires you to master your own thoughts and feelings.

The stakes can be high. You may really want to secure the work, or gain this new client, and be worried about losing out. On the other hand, you also want to agree a price that reflects the true value of your work, and set a powerful precedent for the future. And since your prices are linked with your unique value, it's easy for these thoughts to get tangled up with your sense of self-esteem.

All these factors turn up the emotional heat, which can pull you in many different directions. You might act impulsively, accepting or making proposals that aren't in your best interests. Or you might go to extremes, either by pushing way too hard or by caving in too soon.

Another potential problem is negotiating with yourself, instead of the prospect. In other words, you start second-guessing what the prospect might be thinking or feeling, and modifying your own actions on that basis. For example, you might revise your price downwards before you even send in your proposal, or offer to reduce your price before the prospect has asked you to. Instead, you should only alter the deal in response to what your prospect actually says and does – not what's going on inside your head.

That's why my advice is to keep emotions out of the negotiation as much as you can. I prefer to deal with prospects in writing, since that gives me the time and space to consider my words very carefully, at every stage. If a prospect asks me for a price – or a price cut – when we're on the phone, I *always* ask if I can send them an email later on, even if I'm already 99% sure what I'm going to say.

Use your energy wisely, and sleep on your decision if you can. For example, instead of sending that high-stakes email at 5.30pm – when the prospect probably won't even see it anyway – just leave it until the next morning, when your thinking is bound to be clearer.

Before negotiation starts, it really helps to lay down some ground rules in your mind. That will help you evaluate the prospect's actions in a measured, rational way, without getting blown off course by your own reactions. In the next few sections, we'll look at the key factors you need to consider: your topline, your baseline and the alternatives to striking a deal for both you and your prospect.

35 Set your topline

Your topline is the price you ideally want to get paid for the project. This is the price you will put in your quote, and the starting point for any subsequent negotiations on price. It will reflect the unique value that you will offer on this project, drawing on all the themes we looked at in chapter 3.

At the risk of stating the obvious, your topline is so called because it's the most you can expect to get paid. Very few clients will offer you more – although it does happen sometimes. On your side, you can only really increase your price if new information comes to light later on.

That means it's all downhill from here. Whatever happens next, the only two possible outcomes are that your price is agreed at your topline level, or it comes down. So if you think the prospect is likely to haggle over the price, you need to set your topline at a level that gives you some room to manoeuvre.

Now, at this point, you may start worrying about scaring the prospect off with a high price. Obviously, you want to close the deal and get the work. But at the same time, you must remember that some prospects will simply be unwilling, or unable, to pay you what you're asking for. That's absolutely fine! You don't have to take every job, and selecting the right clients is a really important part of boosting your earnings.

Recall from chapter 2 that you only want to work with clients who meet the BAR. That means your service *benefits* them, they *appreciate* what you do and they have *resources* to spend. If they're falling short on points two and three, it's far better to filter them out right now than get caught up in a tortuous price negotiation or a relationship that's never going to work.

When you lose a job on price, you might hear a voice in your head saying that you could have got it if only your quote had been a *little* lower. But if you'd been in the right ballpark, the prospect would probably have either tried to negotiate, or simply agreed. In reality, they were probably looking for someone far cheaper – so it's just as well they walked away.

A tell-tale sign is when a prospect asks about a different pricing basis, like an hourly rate. This suggests that they are trying to benchmark freelancers against each other on the basis of cost alone. While you can certainly come back with a project price and try to convince them, it's not a very promising start. If they've got their heart set on an hourly-rate deal, they'll surely find one elsewhere. So leave them to it, and refocus on your next good prospect instead.

36 Set your baseline

The counterpart to your topline is your baseline: the lowest price at which you would still accept the project.

Obviously, you don't tell the prospect your baseline, since doing so practically guarantees that you'll get that much and no more. Instead, you keep your baseline inside your head, where you can use it to evaluate any counter-offer the prospect makes.

As long as the prospect's proposed price is still a good way above your baseline, you can consider agreeing to it. If their proposed price is below your baseline, you have two choices: make a counter-offer of your own that's nearer to your topline, or simply walk away.

Remember, your baseline is your absolute last resort, not your first port of call during negotiations. If the prospect invites you to reduce your price, you don't crumple immediately and drop right down to the baseline. Instead, you offer a price cut that looks and sounds significant, but actually keeps you as close as possible to your topline.

I find that a price cut of 10%, explicitly described as such, is hard for prospects to turn down. They asked for a price cut, and now they've got one. Ten per cent is not trivial, but at the same time it's not so big that it implies your first price was complete fantasy. It simply suggests you're paring back your margin to win the client.

If they're still not happy, I think you have a right to politely ask them what price *would* be acceptable, so they have to make a counter-offer. Then it's a simple yes/no question of whether or not that offer is above your baseline.

You can also ask for the prospect's ballpark figure or budget first, to avoid wasting time. However, when it comes to prices, I think most clients expect the provider to show first – and to be honest, that's probably their right. If they reveal their budget up front and you quote a price that's close to it, there will always be the suspicion that you simply tailored your price to suit, and they could have got a better deal if they'd just kept quiet.

Bear in mind that there will be times when you wind up accepting a price that's near your baseline, or even below it. It will probably be when work is thin on the ground, or your confidence is at a low ebb, or both.

Believe me, I've been there. I got my start in freelancing by losing my job, and had to build up from no clients at all. More recently, I plummeted from five-figure months right down to zero when the UK locked down during the pandemic. So I know what it's like to feel completely adrift, with no firm footing to base your pricing on.

If you do a deal you don't like, just mentally put it in a box and leave it there. Sure, it could have been better, but you can't go back. So draw a line under it and move on.

Also, make a decision to confine the mistake to this one client, or this one project. Remember, no-one knows what you're getting paid, so this doesn't have to become a precedent. You can start completely afresh next time.

Knowing what to do is one thing, but actually doing it is another. While the ideas in this chapter are fairly easy to understand, that doesn't mean they're easy to put into practice when you're up against it. So don't beat yourself up for your mistakes – learn from them, and do better next time.

37 Express your price firmly

When communicating your topline price to the prospect, use simple and direct words. Avoid any language that communicates doubt, vagueness or uncertainty.

For example, in your proposal email, say, 'My price to carry out the project on this basis is £250.' Don't weaken your stance by saying that you 'suggest' or 'propose' a price, or muddy the waters by saying 'around £250' or quoting a price range like '£200–£250'.

If you're vague about numbers, you're simply delaying the time when you finally have to confirm your price. And if you express ambivalence, you're just inviting the prospect to try and knock you down a bit. You're also implying a lack of confidence in your own skills, which might even make them rethink whether they want to use you.

This is a decision point for both you and the prospect, and it needs to be understood as such. You make a clear offer, and they make a clear decision to buy. There's no going back.

38 Know your BATNA

Sometimes, trying to win a project can feel like 'all or nothing'. You're either going to get this project or you're not. If you get it, you'll have some work – great! But if you don't get it, you'll have *nada*. If you work on a lot of short timescales, like I do, a single order could make the difference between a solid week of work and tumbleweeds.

We all hate to lose, and that strong emotion can affect our decisions. Psychologists call it *loss aversion*. Thanks to loss aversion, you already feel anxious about losing a potential job, even though you haven't even won it yet.

Basically, losing would be painful. So, to try and avoid that pain, you dial down your price target or agree to some sort of discount, to boost your chances of landing the deal. By running away from an emotional loss, you run towards a financial one. You're negotiating with yourself – and losing.

The antidote to this downward spiral is to identify your BATNA. The initials stand for *Best Alternative to a Negotiated Agreement*, and the concept was developed by negotiation researchers Roger Fisher and William Ury of the Harvard Program on Negotiation.[4]

Basically, your BATNA is whatever you will do if this deal doesn't pan out. It's your 'next best thing' to winning the business.

Your BATNA could be business-focused. It might just be working for another client. Or you could search out some more prospects and do some marketing. You could improve your skills by taking a course or attending an event. You could work up some social media posts, or even start writing your book. Then again, maybe it's time to break out of your office for a swim, run, hike or whatever else makes you feel good.

The crucial point about your BATNA is that it exists. It is not nothing. If you don't win this business, you *will* have

---

[4] Read more about it in their landmark book on negotiation, *Getting to Yes* (Baker & Taylor, 2011).

something – even if it's only the time, energy and opportunity to do something else. Plus you will have learned something from this episode that will help you in the future – because just about *every* freelancing experience contains a valuable lesson of one sort or another.

Your BATNA highlights the fact that you *always* have other options; you *always* have a choice. It reminds you that winning this one project is not the be-all and end-all of your career, even though it might feel that way right now. If this doesn't work out, you'll just go and do something else until the next good opportunity comes along.

So, before you propose your price, identify your BATNA, and imagine in detail what you'll do as an alternative to this work. Having done that, you'll either close the deal at the right level, or embrace the alternative with a sense of purpose and positive choice.

39 Know your prospect's BATNA

Just as you have a BATNA, so does your prospect. And it helps to know it – or, at least, to try and work out what it might be.

Your prospect's BATNA is the mirror image of yours. It's whatever they will do if they can't reach an agreement with you, for whatever reason.

Since freelancers are generally easy to find, the prospect's BATNA will probably be to go back to the market and choose someone else. However, if you offer specialist expertise, or if you have specific experience of this type of project, that option might be less appealing to them.

On a softer level, they might have just taken a shine to you, or already reached a semi-conscious decision that they want to use you – something you may be able to detect in their words or manner. So while they do have a BATNA, technically speaking, that doesn't necessarily mean they feel good about using it.

The more you've interacted with the prospect about the project so far, the clearer the picture they will have of the value you offer. So the more effort you put into presenting your prices (chapter 4), the better you look in comparison to their BATNA.

A similar point applies if the prospect found you through a recommendation. Right off the bat, you are a known quantity that their trusted friend or colleague has recommended by name. They feel that they know you already, plus some of the referrer's goodwill rubs off on you. You're halfway home already.

In contrast, their BATNA could be someone completely unknown who they must go out and research for themselves. And they clearly don't feel confident about doing that, or they wouldn't have asked for a recommendation in the first place. The very best they can hope for is their pal's second-choice recommendation – because *you* were the first.

If the project has a crunchy deadline, time is not on the prospect's side. The longer they spend talking to you about the project, the less time they have to find a backup if the deal falls through. This is particularly salient if the project is long and complex, so it takes a certain amount of time just to explain it and obtain a quote. Basically, the prospect's BATNA is getting less and less appealing by the day, while yours stays pretty much the same – or even improves, if some other work turns up in the meantime. (However, you should always act in good faith; don't be tempted to exploit the situation by deliberately stalling.)

All these points, plus any others you can think of, can help you to clarify the true balance of power between you and the prospect. While they do have authority in terms of deciding whether or not to use you, that doesn't mean they have the power to boss every aspect of the relationship.

When you think about it, the prospect's BATNA might not be all that great – and the worse it is, the less likely they are to walk away. That can give you more confidence to set a higher price to begin with, or to call the prospect's bluff if your price comes under pressure.

Obviously, a lot of this will be based on deduction. You can never really know what's going through your prospect's mind. However, there's one thing you *can* be sure of: they want to use *you*. They looked at the options available, and they chose *you*. Yes, they can use someone else, but that will always be their second-best choice. For the moment, you are in the driver's seat.

40 Don't play pipeline

Sometimes, prospects will try to agree an 'introductory' discount on the basis of 'lots of work in the pipeline' or 'the start of a long-lasting relationship'. So what they're hoping for is a bulk discount, but without actually ordering in bulk.

Of course, you'd *love* to have a bulging pipeline of future work from a longstanding, loyal client. That's precisely why this tactic is so powerful, so seductive. But even with the best will in the world, these good intentions don't always pan out. Over the course of my career, I've worked with several clients who started out talking big, only to fade away after one or two jobs.

What happened? Maybe their plans and circumstances changed. Maybe my service didn't help them as much as they hoped. Or maybe they just felt like a change. It doesn't really matter. The crucial lesson is that, unfortunately, you simply cannot take prospects' stated plans or timescales at face value. The risk to your own business is just too great.

The other possibility, of course, is that your prospect is just trying to secure a discount from you now by pointing to a pipeline that doesn't even exist, and never will. In that case, you *definitely* want to steer clear. This is a pure power play, designed to extract a concession from you at the outset and set the tone for everything that happens later on.

Your starting point should always be to discount on *real and present work only*. If a prospect tries a pipeline play, you can avoid saying a blunt 'no' by responding that you're happy to offer bulk discounts on confirmed projects, or something like that. In effect, you're saying, 'OK then, show me the work,' but framing it in more polite, constructive way.

Bear in mind, though, that they *may* actually come up with the goods, in which case you are committed to offering at least a token discount (like 10%). Also, if they are unscrupulous enough to play pipeline, they may also be prepared to rustle up a bunch of 'vapourwork' that is supposedly ready to start, but never actually goes ahead.

On the other hand, some prospects genuinely have a long list of things they want done, and will ask you in good faith to quote for everything up front. That's great. However, it does oblige you to spend a fair amount of time thinking through a lot of projects and prices, with no guarantee that *any* of them will go ahead.

So, in this situation, I sometimes ask if I can quote for, and work on, one specific smaller project first, before we look at the rest of the stuff. That way, we can establish that my pricing, approach and final results are all acceptable before we launch into tons of work. Prospects usually agree to this quite readily, because they can see that it reduces risk for them too.

41 Do paid samples, not free ones

A similar approach to the introductory discount is the free sample. Prospects will ask for one because they 'need to see what you can do for us'. Free samples are the bane of the creative industries, but I'm sure freelancers in other sectors suffer the same problem too.

Obviously, the risk for you is that you put time and effort into the sample, but still lose out on the work. If you're just starting out, you might feel that's a gamble worth taking. If you don't get the gig, you can justify the sample as a marketing overhead, or a way to sharpen your skills and build up a portfolio. You do free work now, so you can get paid work later.

However, once you've been freelancing for a while, your portfolio should give prospects a clear enough picture of what you can do. The request for a free sample is really just a power play. The whole point is that the prospect makes a demand that you comply with.

On a practical level, the main problem with free samples is that you're usually working in a vacuum. So you may be given a narrow, fairly specific assignment – perhaps an excerpt from a larger project – without any real knowledge of what the prospect's business is all about.

Indeed, this may be precisely the intention: to throw you in at the deep end and see whether you sink or swim. But without context, you're flying blind, and there's just no way you can do your best work.

By asking for free samples, the prospect hopes to avoid wasting time on briefing someone who isn't right for them, or paying for work they don't like. But they can't really tell who's a good fit, or obtain any decent output, until they get into the work for real. When it comes to building great working relationships, there really are no short cuts.

Just as aptitude tests in job interviews are not like real work, so free samples are not a true reflection of the way freelancers collaborate with their clients. They're just a blunt instrument to assess one aspect of your ability. Cast your mind back to chapter 3, when we explored the many dimensions of value you can offer, and consider how few of them are actually covered by a sample.

What's more, by taking on a free sample, you will give yourself what economists call a *perverse incentive* – because you'll be focused on winning the work, rather than delivering true value. Since you won't have any real insight into what the prospect wants or needs, you'll try to impress them as best you can, in the hope of winning the business. You won't challenge any problems with the brief, for fear of rocking the boat. But that will give a misleading impression of what your service is really like.

Overall, a free sample is so unrepresentative that it's not really a 'sample' at all. It's more like a laboratory experiment that bears very little relation to real life. And that's why it's simply not productive for you or the prospect.

Therefore, if a prospect asks you to do a free sample, you could counter-offer by giving your quote to do the sample on a paid basis. Include some research and thinking time (see chapter 3) to show that you regard these as an integral part of any project. You might be surprised how many clients back down when their bluff is called this way, and agree to pay at least *something* to see what you can do. You can then proceed on a basis of mutual trust and respect, instead of a one-sided power play.

42 Trade time for money

The two factors that are most likely to figure in your negotiations are money and time. If the prospect wants the work super quick, they are not really in a position to dictate terms on price as well.

So you should be able to hold firm on the price if they are making tough time demands.

In some circumstances, you may even be able to increase your price, by proposing a premium for quick delivery. However, I advise caution, because this may ramp up the prospect's expectations of quality, to the point where you can't actually meet them in the time you have. It might be wiser just to say that you'll do your best within the time available, and stick with your usual pricing.

As a general rule, always give worst-case timescales. It's always better to under-promise and over-deliver – plus it makes for a more relaxed and civilized freelance lifestyle all round. However, it also gives you room to manoeuvre if the client requests quicker delivery and you can see an opportunity to tweak the deal to your advantage.

When setting timescales, watch out for factors you can't control. For example, I often write articles based on phone interviews with my client's own customers. They're great fun to do, but the interviewees can sometimes be hard to get hold of. So I make it clear to the client that my own timescale depends on the interviewee's availability, and specify it in relative rather than absolute terms. For example, I'll promise 'First draft within five working days of the interview' rather than 'First draft by April 5th'.

43 Trade money for time

Conversely, if the timescale is more relaxed, you might agree to a lower price in order to buy more time – but *only* if it makes sense for you.

When does it make sense? Basically, whenever you can use your extra time to make more money elsewhere. If you can quickly do another project with a short timescale, *and* take this one too, that could be a smart move in terms of your overall income and work scheduling.

The downside is the same as with all discounts: setting an unwelcome precedent. Say your client comes back with a similar project later on, and asks if they can have the same price again. However unfair that request might be, it will still be up to you to raise an objection, or just put up with it. As we saw in chapter 3, you always want precedents to work for you, not against you.

44 Trade money for convenience

If your client requests a discount on a larger or more complex project, you may be able to reduce the price in return for making the project easier to handle.

For example, I'm sometimes asked to quote for writing a set of articles or blog posts – say 15. Nominally, it's a single project – but I know from experience that the individual elements often end up drifting apart. I might get some of the article briefs ahead of others, or the feedback might arrive piecemeal, or the scope might change during the project, or I might end up having to invoice for part of the work before the rest.

As we saw in chapter 3, all that project-management stuff soaks up time and effort. All the loose ends have to be tied up with emails or phone calls, and I'll often have to create my own project spreadsheet just to keep track of what's going on.

Now, normally, you would set a topline price that covers contingencies like this, or explicitly includes project management. Ideally, your price represents the level at which you're happy to see the project through, come what may. But if you agree to a bulk discount and the project then falls to pieces, you're stuck between a rock and a hard place, dealing with more hassle for less money.

So, if valued clients ask me for a bulk discount on jobs like this, I offer one – but with strings attached. To return to the example above, I might stipulate that all the articles must be briefed, written, reviewed, approved and invoiced as a unit. That means I don't start until I have *all* the stuff, I submit all the text in a single, all-encompassing document and I expect the feedback to be provided in one go and fully collated (that is, with no internal contradictions or open questions). And when the work is done, I'll send a single invoice that covers everything.

I might also stipulate that I'll only deal with one person within the client organization. That makes sure I don't end up chasing approvals from people who aren't invested in the project and have no idea who I am.

Or I might propose that I'll only carry out one round of changes, instead of my usual two. Terms like these keep the client on point when it comes to feedback, when they might otherwise let changes slide until later on.

Provided the client sticks to the deal, that arrangement should keep a lid on my project-management overhead and make sure the whole thing is still worthwhile. The only possible downside is that by insisting that everything is rigidly bolted together, I end up slowing the whole project down. For instance, despite our best efforts, me and my contact might still end up waiting for one pesky foot-dragger to send in their feedback, leaving me frustratingly unable to invoice. But at least I've set out what I want to happen in principle, and got my contact's explicit agreement on it. If nothing else, I've got the right to complain if things get messy.

Actually, this kind of condition can be worth including even if you're not negotiating, because clients don't always appreciate that separating or reordering elements can have a big impact on you. For instance, if you were planning to work on two things in parallel, but the client says, 'I'll brief you on the other bit when you've finished the first,' the project might suddenly become less attractive to you. But since you're already into the hands-on work, you might find it hard to impose your own preference without looking unreasonable.

45 Reduce scope, not price

Another factor you can bring into the deal is the scope of the project itself. In simple terms, instead of agreeing to do the whole job for less, you counter-offer that you'll do part of the job for a partial fee that's in line with your original quote. For example, a copy-editor might offer to work on the main text of a book or article, but not the index or the references.

This approach is a win-win for both sides. You get to bring the client on board and start working with them, but without compromising on price. And if things go well, they may ask you to do the rest of the job anyway.

For their part, the client gets to see what you can do for them, but with a reduced financial commitment. It's a similar arrangement to the paid samples I mentioned above, except that this work is definitely part of the project at hand, not a specially developed test.

However, there are three important caveats to this approach. First, it only really works if the project can be easily broken down into chunks – or, at least, that there's one chunk you can break off and do first. Otherwise, you can run into the same issue we saw with samples: nobody can do their best work in a vacuum.

Second, bear in mind that for some projects, a lot of the effort in terms of project management, research or planning might be front-loaded towards the start, and you might have to do most or all of that work before you can start to produce anything useful.

So if you agree to deliver, say, one-fifth of the final product, you can't assume that it will take one-fifth of the time and effort. Plus you might have nearly as much to-ing and fro-ing over email as you would if you did the whole thing. Therefore, you shouldn't just pro rata your original price by one-fifth. Or, if you do, be aware that this really constitutes a discount for the client, and that it's not such a good deal for you if the main project never goes ahead.

Finally, dividing up the work creates natural break-points in the project, and these bring risks for you. The major one is the client simply deciding not to go any further. However, they could also delay, change the scope or even try to revisit the price. You need to weigh the risk of these uncertainties against the benefit of winning the client.

46 Use anchoring

This is a way to make your price seem lower in the eyes of a prospect.

The idea is that we think of prices (or other amounts) as smaller when we've heard a higher amount first. Basically, everything's relative.

Imagine you're visiting an online clothing store in search of a nice shirt. The first one you see is £250, while the second one is £125. Now, in your mind, the £125 shirt is somehow 'cheap' – even though £125 might still be far more than you'd normally pay for a shirt.

The £250 acts as an 'anchor' that fixes your price expectations in a certain range. Once you've heard the anchor, you can't help comparing whatever you hear afterwards with it.

The first number acts as a frame or lens through which you see other numbers.

There are a couple of ways you can use anchoring.

If you're in conversation with a prospect and they ask about prices, you could quote a rate from the top of the market before telling them yours. For example, 'A digital marketing agency would probably charge you around 10 thousand to build a 10-page site, but I normally come in around three or four thousand.'

Remember, your upper price anchor needs to be both honest and plausible. You can't just pluck a number out of the air, because the prospect might do their own research. You also need to make sure you're quoting a price from someone that the prospect might be reasonably expected to use. If they could never afford the alternative price anyway, or would never think of using that type of provider, your anchor won't be so effective.

By the same token, the technique may not work as well on people who have more knowledge of your industry, or have bought your type of service many times before. If they already have a frame of reference firmly established in their minds, your anchor probably won't be strong enough to disrupt it. They may also see through it as a persuasive trick, because they don't really need any information from you to support their choice. So choose your targets carefully, and only use the technique if you feel comfortable with it.

One frame of reference that works well for some freelancers is geographical. If you are based out in the sticks, you can put your prices in a favourable light by comparing them to rates from London, New York or wherever. Freelancers who've previously worked in a major centre, but then relocated, can use a subtler version of this, like 'Big-city skills at small-town prices.' However, this will only work if you know your prospect would actually consider using a provider from the big city, and appreciates the way prices can vary from one area to another.

Another approach is to quote a higher price for a bunch of tasks or services, then a lower price for all of them together. For example, you might say that you'd normally charge £150 to build a dining chair, or £900 for a set of six – but you'll discount the full set to £600. It's just a bulk discount; nothing fancy. But it's a way to fix a high anchor in the prospect's mind, and suggest that you've saved them £300 (or whatever) right off the bat. As an alternative, you could keep the discount in your pocket, and pull it out to use on prospects who are hesitating.

Again, your upper price must not sound fabricated. For example, people selling online learning will sometimes say that the elements of a £500 course 'would cost £2000 if bought separately,' or something similar. But if they're not even *available* separately, the claim is rather hollow. Both your unit price and your discounted bulk price should be genuine – or at least *feel* genuine to the prospect.

47 Don't split the difference

When you submit your price, your prospect may come back with a counter-offer. Or, if they reveal a (low) budget initially, you may come back with your own (higher) price. Either way, you end up with two potential prices on the table, which you somehow need to bridge if you're going to reach a deal.

One option, which your prospect may suggest, is to split the difference – that is, settle on a price halfway between your two respective offers. If they said they'd pay £200, and your proposed price was £600, splitting the difference means shaking hands on £400.

It *looks* fair and even-handed, doesn't it? But although those two prices may just look like two neutral numbers, they actually represent two very different things.

Your price has been carefully worked out to reflect the value of the work, in all its dimensions (chapter 3). But the prospect's offer may have no facts or consideration behind it at all. It's just a number that they're throwing out there in the hope of saving themselves some cash. And while you're trying to strike a deal in good faith, they may be prepared to do and say pretty much anything to get a discount, safe in the knowledge that if their plan fails, they can just walk away.

In terms of negotiation mechanics, the prospect may be making their offer purely to establish a low anchor and pull your price expectations downwards, in a way that mirrors the anchoring technique we saw just above. Having done that, they can then offer to 'split the difference' and get the price they were hoping to pay all along. House purchasers can play similar games when they're making offers for properties in a buyer's market.

Now, you may feel that anyone using this tactic is just trying to play you, and that you should just turn their work down flat. I wouldn't blame you if you did.

If you do decide to soldier on, make sure you evaluate the 'split difference' price on the right terms. The prospect isn't really giving you anything by offering to split the difference; they're just framing their counter-offer in a certain way. On your side, however, splitting the difference may represent a serious discount that you wouldn't otherwise offer. So if the resulting price falls below your baseline, this project may not be right for you.

On the other hand, if your topline was strong, and the prospect's counter-offer wasn't outrageous, the 'split difference' price might actually be OK. If so, you may feel happy to go ahead, as long as you don't feel too manipulated and you're content to set a price precedent at this level. This shows the importance of getting your topline right from the outset, to give yourself some elbow room. Prospects can play all the games all they want – as long as *you* set the rules.

48 Use bigness bias

Bigness bias refers to the way smaller amounts seem insignificant in the context of larger ones. It's similar to anchoring, but instead of comparing your price to one that the prospect probably *won't* pay, you compare it to something else that they probably *are* paying, or plausibly could.

For example, a £600 fee for a property survey might sound like a lot for some guy with a clipboard to look round a house. But if you're buying a property for £250,000, and plan to live in it for 20 years, the survey starts to look like a smart purchase.

As you can see, the key to bigness bias is to link your price with another *relevant* amount in order to make it sound smaller. For example, you could say, 'An e-commerce website usually costs at least £25,000, so £1500 to get the right content is a no-brainer.'

Using bigness bias in a face-to-face discussion takes guts, since you need to (a) raise the fact that the client is spending money elsewhere, which is none of your business, and (b) take a stab at guessing how much. If you make a wrong assumption, the ploy will fail, and you'll look foolish into the bargain. So this tactic might be better suited to a blog post or a page on your website, like an FAQ, where you can frame the scenario as a general illustration rather than an intrusive observation about a specific client.

49 Put your price in context

Techniques such as anchoring or bigness bias aim to make your price look smaller in the context of other prices. Another approach is to bring in other aspects of the client's context (chapter 3) in order to make the price seem less significant. For example, you could refer to:

- *Time*. Either the prospect is spending a lot of time on this project, or they stand to save a lot of time. For example, 'If you're spending all those hours in the gym, you want to see a real gain. With my personal training, you will.'

- *Effort*. Similarly, the prospect is either putting in a lot of effort, or could save themselves a lot of hassle. For example, 'Lawn care is back-breaking work with no guarantee of success. Give yourself a break and get an expert instead.'

- *Irrevocability*. The buying decision is difficult or impossible to reverse or redo, so it's vital to get everything right first time. For example, 'Your wedding is a once-in-a-lifetime occasion, so you want to get it right. My planning service takes care of every detail.'

Maybe you can't imagine yourself saying things like this out loud. But you could still use them in marketing materials such as your website, or maybe in emails to the prospect.

With all these techniques, you highlight potential problems of *not* using you. You then 'poke' the problems to make them sound really bad and portray your service as the safe and reassuring option. In the process, you frame the cost as 'a price worth paying' to make the problem go away.

However, just because you get the prospect fleeing from a problem, that doesn't necessarily mean they will run into your arms. You also need to make a positive case for why they should choose you *specifically*. Otherwise, you can wind up making the generic case for using freelancers like you without actually closing the sale for yourself. To reel the prospect in, give them *specific* details of the value you offer, who your clients are and the results you've achieved.

Incidentally, this kind of 'generic selling' is a characteristic problem with freelancers' marketing. Instead of selling themselves specifically, they sell the service they offer in the most general terms. For example, their home page opens with 'Why you should use a proofreader,' or something similar. The prospect already knows that they need the service, or they wouldn't be Googling it in the first place. Your job is not to tell your prospects that bread tastes good; it's to sell them the loaf that you have baked.

50 Act as if

I once received an enquiry email from a prospect during a hideously busy period. In fact, I was so snowed under that I had half a mind to turn them down flat. But instead, I submitted a 'get lost price', fully expecting them to reject it and save me the trouble of 'firing' them.

But they didn't. They agreed right away, and asked when I could get started.

Only then did I finally Google their company name, and discover they were a major multinational, literally a thousand times larger than I'd imagined. What's more, they became one of my most consistent and valued clients – and all at the 'get lost' price level, too.

One lesson from this story is that you should always know who you're talking to. But if I *had* known that, I probably wouldn't have acted the same way, which means I might not have achieved the same outcome. So another lesson is that 'acting as if' can be very powerful.

What I mean is that vividly imagining yourself in a position of power can allow you to act from that power, even if you don't necessarily possess it. If you can get yourself into the headspace of someone who doesn't really need the work, your negotiating position is far stronger. I imagined my prospect was a minnow instead of a whale, and that ignorance actually gave me strength.

Alternatively, if it's not too stressful, you could imagine that you have something else more important outside work that's weighing on your mind right now. You have a lot of important things in your life, and work is just one of them. So you want the project, but not at any price. And you certainly don't have time to mess around. It's your way or the highway.

Negotiators sometimes express this idea as 'She who cares least wins.' Whoever has the least to lose – or *feels* they have the least to lose – is in the strongest position.

It's the same mentality you need to pull off a daring bluff in poker. If your play convinces your opponent that you're holding aces, and you don't particularly care what they've got, you can get them to fold based on perception alone.

Maybe you'll find it hard to act like a boss when in reality you're short of work. But if nothing else, you can use this technique to bolster your self-image and stop yourself from self-sabotaging. Think of yourself as a professional, in-demand service provider – *which you are* – and act out of that image. Otherwise, you'll go into a spiral of falling confidence and falling prices, each one reinforcing the other.

This technique is well established in neuro-linguistic programming (NLP) as a way to learn quickly and intuitively. Instead of painstakingly acquiring knowledge through book learning or experience, you simply observe someone who already has the skill you want, then model yourself on them as best you can. Who could you use as a role model for your freelance pricing and deal-making?

51 Use 'feel, felt, found'

This is a technique you can use to overcome a specific price objection that you know prospects might raise. It takes the form of three sentences that you write or speak in sequence.

First, you acknowledge that the prospect is thinking or feeling a certain way – in this case, that they have a price objection. That's the 'feel'.

Second, you reveal that other people you know used to feel the same way as the prospect. That's the 'felt' part. The 'others' are probably other clients you've worked for in the past, but they can be anybody that the prospect could identify with.

Finally, you explain that those others went on to have some experience, or discovered some knowledge, that changed the way they felt – in this case, that they dropped their price objections. That's the 'found'.

Let's say your prospect is questioning whether your design service is really worth the price. You could respond:

> *I understand how you <u>feel</u>. Many of my longstanding clients once <u>felt</u> the same way. But they <u>found</u> that when they bought cheap design, they had to ask someone with more experience to redo it later on.*

In psychological terms, 'feel, felt, found' works with a combination of empathy and social proof.

The 'feel' part shows empathy, because you recognize what the prospect is feeling, and acknowledge it as valid. It shows them that you're not going to try to dismiss it, or override it, or argue them out of their position. You give them 'psychological air'.

Then, 'felt' adds another dimension by bringing in social proof. Other people used to feel the same way, so the prospect feels vindicated. However, this also opens the door to exploring those other people's experience, using shared emotions as a key.

Finally, 'found' carries the prospect forward in time, to what will happen if they stay with their current mindset. It turns social proof around, to say that although others have been this way before, ultimately it was the wrong path. So if the prospect still identifies with them, and wants to do what they did, they need to abandon their objection.

You're most likely to use 'feel, felt, found' in writing – for example, in an FAQ page on your website, or maybe as the basis for a social media post about pricing in your industry. However, if you prepare your response carefully, and the right opportunity comes up, you may feel confident enough to use it in conversation with a prospect.

52 Walk away

If you feel the prospect is asking for too many concessions, or just messing you about, you might decide to stop trying to cater to them and just walk away. After all, there comes a point where your time would be better spent on trying to convert a different prospect.

If so, be polite, not rude or dismissive. Say something like, 'Sorry, but this isn't working out. I think you would be better off working with someone else.'

How will the prospect respond? Some will just shrug, accept your decision and move on. Some may be affronted, and demand to know why their business isn't good enough for you. However, for others, being 'fired' acts as a wake-up call. They realize that they are at fault, their BATNA is not so great and they really don't want to lose the chance to work with you. So they immediately shape up, drop the game-playing and agree to your terms.

In other words, walking away from a deal can *sometimes* be the best way to close it. (Double underlining on that *sometimes*.) However, as a tactic to win the business, it's *extremely* risky, and it requires you to make two vital calls.

The first question is whether you're happy to run the risk of losing out on the project, and irritating the prospect, on the off-chance of making them see the light.

It's not so bad if they just storm off – that's between you and them, and it goes no further. But if they get really riled up, there's always a slim chance that they could badmouth you to their friends and colleagues, or post a negative review of your business online. That's why it's so important to be civil and courteous at all times, however tough your underlying stance may be.

If the prospect does come round, the second question is whether you actually want to go ahead, given the way things have gone down so far. You should only proceed if you truly believe things will be different from now on. Can you and the prospect both move on from these rather tense negotiations, and build a strong relationship regardless? If so, go right ahead.

Takeaways from this chapter

- Know your topline, baseline and BATNA before you negotiate. Think about your prospect's BATNA too.
- Only offer discounts on real and present work. As a rule, don't do free samples or offer discounts for vapourwork.

- Bring in other dimensions – such as scope, time and convenience – to reach agreement without compromising on price.
- Reframe your price to make it look more affordable, or good value in context. Be aware of framing tactics that prospects may use on you, such as 'split the difference'.
- Be prepared to walk away.

6 INCREASING YOUR PRICES

'Put your prices up' seems like obvious advice – but as many freelancers find, it isn't always that simple. This chapter looks at some smarter ways to increase your prices.

53 Don't work more, charge more

Increasing your prices means you earn more money. That's great. But just as importantly, it can prevent you from overworking yourself, letting down your clients and ultimately undermining your own success.

If your prices are set too low, you might try to compensate by simply taking on more work. The logic here can be quite seductive. For example, if you work an eight-hour day, adding on just 48 minutes' extra work at the end of every day increases your output by 10%, which could theoretically boost your earnings by 10% as well. Most salaried workers would be pleased to get a raise like that.

So far, so good. But the problem is that nothing comes for free. It's nine to five, five days a week for a reason: your brain, and even your body, can only do so much. While you can probably fit in a few extra hours here and there, it's not really sustainable. And you clearly can't keep adding more and more hours indefinitely.

You're not a machine. You need time to recuperate so you can do your best work. If you keep trying to push the needle into the red, quality will inevitably start to go downhill. As tiredness and overwork take their toll, you'll probably start forgetting things or making mistakes, and letting clients down in the process.

If you're young and confident enough, you might be able to style it out and gloss over a few slip-ups here and there. But take it from me: the older you get, the more sieve-like your brain becomes – and the more significant, and embarrassing, these lapses are. You're expected to be a wise old bird, but you're acting more like a headless chicken. It really isn't a good look.

If any of this does happen to you, it will make it *harder* to increase your prices, not easier. Instead of basing your increases on a solid record of quality work, you'll be looking back and asking yourself whether you're really worth that higher rate. And your clients might be asking themselves the same thing.

By filling up every available hour with hands-on work, you're also taking time away from other activities that could help you boost your earnings, like learning new skills or marketing yourself. Instead of sharpening the saw, you're blunting your edge through overwork.

So although working longer hours might bring you a small financial gain in the short term, you could sacrifice a much larger, more sustainable gain over the long term. You're getting cash today, but at the expense of true wealth tomorrow.

And that's why you need to charge more – not just work more.

54 Charge new clients more

It's far easier to quote a higher price for a new client than to increase the price you charge an existing one. So whenever you're putting together a price for a potential new client, consider whether you could charge them more than you've been charging your existing clients for the same work.

This is particularly important if you're already busy most of the time. If you already have a full roster of clients, there's really no point in taking on more at the exact same price level. You're simply piling more pressure on yourself.

You're also putting yourself in the position where you'll have to prioritize between clients, while denying yourself the simplest, most objective measure to do so. OK, you might not *always* favour your best-paying clients – but you'll probably need a good reason not to.

So instead of going down that road, make it easy on yourself by bringing new clients on board at higher prices. Once they're established as regulars who are happy to pay at that level, that will give you the security to raise the rates for your other existing clients to the same level. Use new clients to add new rungs at the top of your price ladder, which the others can then climb up.

Even if you don't succeed in doing that, your earnings should still gradually increase, simply through the natural process of losing and gaining clients over time (known as 'churn'). Newer, higher-paying clients join, while older, lower-paying ones drift away.

Obviously, this implies charging different rates to different clients for the same kind of work. Personally, I think that's fine; you're free to charge whatever you want, to whoever you want, whenever you want. But if you're uncomfortable with it – or if you're worried about your clients talking to each other, maybe – you need to keep all your existing clients at the same level, and increase them all in one go. So let's look at how you can do that.

55   Increase prices for existing clients

Sounds obvious, right? If you want to make more money, just put your prices up. Head over LinkedIn and you'll see dozens of posts urging freelancers and consultants to charge more.

But while raising your rates may seem like a no-brainer, many freelancers still have trouble actually doing it. And I certainly include myself in that.

How about you? When did you last increase your prices across the board? Was it as easy as all those excitable blog posts implied? Or did you find yourself making a few exceptions here and there, or maybe waiting a little longer than you needed to?

There's no two ways about it. Increasing prices can feel disruptive and risky. The fear of rocking the boat and losing clients is strong. And that means that the temptation to leave things as they are is also strong.

As we saw in chapter 3, precedents are your friends – but after a certain amount of time, they can also become your enemies. Once you've got a client locked in at a particular price, it's safe and comfortable to let your prices ride – particularly if you've gained some additional clients at a higher price point in the meantime. Now you've got some cash cows, maybe you can let sleeping dogs lie.

The problem is you can end up with a base of 'legacy' clients who are very loyal and valued, but are now paying way below your going rate. Therefore, you really should be looking to bring your older clients up to the same level as new ones, if you can. After all, if your newer clients are willing to pay that rate, why not the older ones too?

Some options for increasing your prices include:

- Simply quoting a higher price than you did before for the same sort of work

- Switching from a less desirable pricing model to a more desirable one (for example, from time-based pricing to project pricing – see chapter 3)
- Bringing more elements into your prices (see chapter 3). For example, maybe you never charged for meetings before, but now you're going to start
- Increasing the rates you charge for time-based tasks or fixed-price packages (see chapter 7).

Now, some clients may demand to know why the price you're quoting them today is so different from the one you charged them a month ago. That can be uncomfortable, but it's important to stand firm.

The simplest answer is that you've increased your prices, full stop. As I just argued, you're completely at liberty to charge whatever you want. What's more, unless you signed a contract, you have no legal or moral obligation to hold your prices at a particular level. Clients may grumble, but at the end of the day, you set your price, and they can take it or leave it.

However, if you really value a particular client, you might not want them to leave it. The obvious case would be if they are one of your two or three biggest clients, who account for a significant proportion of your annual earnings. You'd rather have their continuing business – even if its value is declining in real terms – than risk losing the whole lot over a price increase and having to scramble to replace it.

If you're worried about that, maybe you can strike a deal with them to pay at least *little* more. As we saw in chapter 5, 'splitting the difference' isn't usually a smart play. But maybe you *could* offer to split the difference between your current and proposed prices. At least you're splitting the difference on your own numbers – not the client's random suggestion. So if you feel it's worth sacrificing 50% of your proposed price increase in order to retain this client, go ahead. The more ambitious your proposed increase is, the less painful it will be to give up half of it.

We saw in chapter 3 how project-based pricing is the best approach. And when you come to increase prices, you realize why.

I use a daily rate for a couple of clients, basically for historical reasons (those precedents again). When I've increased that rate, I've felt duty bound to let my clients know before I do any work at the higher level, because the existing rate does feel like a commitment. For me, saying 'This is my daily rate' does signify *some* sort of agreement, however loose and informal.

In contrast, when you quote each project separately, it's far easier to gently nudge up the price without making a big song and dance about it. The fact that you priced a project at a certain level before doesn't imply any commitment to offer that price again. So when a new price request comes in, you simply quote at the new rate, without necessarily drawing attention to it. Or, if the client is clearly expecting the price for a particular type of project to be in line with a previous precedent, you just neutrally point out that, actually, this price has now changed.

56   Think through what could happen

Even when you feel fully justified in increasing your prices, it can still be a scary thing to do. In my experience, this fear is powerful but hazy: you're worried that something bad might happen, but you're not that clear on what it might be. So let's take a minute to think through all the possible outcomes when you raise the price on a client.

- First, the client might *express an opinion* about the increase. Even though this is actually the least consequential outcome, it could still be the one you feel most apprehensive about, depending on the client's personality and your own. The client's opinion might be negative – for example, the raise is too much, or it's happening too soon, or it doesn't fit with their budget. Or they might even get personal, by saying something like 'Wow, you drive a hard bargain!' To maintain perspective, consciously separate the client's reactions and observations from the concrete details of what they actually want, or say they're going to do. Also, remember that you can acknowledge their opinion without agreeing with it (for example, 'Thanks for your feedback'). They may not have put a lot of thought into their reaction; it may be something they feel they just have to say, without necessarily acting on.

- In concrete terms, the most likely outcome is that the client simply *accepts* the increase – regardless of what they think or say about it. On a human level, they may agree that you deserve some reward for all your hard work. So thank them for accepting the raise.

- If the client isn't happy about the higher price, they might **make a counter-offer**. If so, you respond exactly as you would during a new-business negotiation (chapter 5). Your topline is the new rate you're aiming for, and your baseline falls, say, halfway between that and what you're getting now. If the client's counter-offer is high enough, you can accept it. However, bear in mind that this might set a precedent that any future increases are up for negotiation too.

- If the client grumbles without actually proposing anything, you could **offer a slightly smaller increase**. As we saw in chapter 5, a price cut of 10% feels significant, but won't be such a great sacrifice as long as your topline is ambitious enough. Again, bear in mind that the client may take this as a precedent, and adopt a strategy of 'Complain to get 10% off' from now on.

- If negotiations fail, or don't happen at all, the client might **refuse to accept any increase**. You then have to decide whether or not to back down.

    - If you want to stand firm, you must *fire the client*. Say something like, 'I'm sorry, I can't meet your expectations on price this time. But thanks for considering me.' This is a polite way of saying, 'If you won't pay what I'm asking, forget it.' Now, up to this point, the client may not have fully understood or accepted that this would happen if they said no to the increase. So they might rethink their position when they realize that you are for real. But equally, they might just shrug and walk away.

    - If you *really* don't want to lose the client, you can **abandon your increase** and agree to continue at the existing rate. You're giving ground to the client and setting a very unwelcome precedent, but at least you haven't lost anything concrete. What's more, you've sent a clear signal that you want to increase your prices sooner or later. Maybe you could agree with the client to revisit the issue in six months. By that time, you might have gained some other business that puts you in a stronger negotiating position.

- As an alternative to all the above, it's also possible that the client might not negotiate, or even respond to your demand, and simply **walk away**. But in my experience, you'll usually have at least some opportunity for discussion and negotiation before they take this step.

That's pretty much everything that could go down. Admittedly, some of these outcomes are better than others, but none of them is disastrous. The absolute worst that can happen is that you lose a single client – and that loss will not destroy your freelance business, unless you are utterly dependent on them.

If you're still worried about clients jumping ship, recall some of the themes we covered earlier on. As we saw in chapter 3, once clients appreciate your unique value, they generally want to stay loyal. You are a known and trusted partner, while their BATNA (chapter 5) is fraught with risk: returning to the market and working with a complete stranger at an unknown cost. So while it may seem to you that the client can easily walk away, it actually creates quite a few problems for them. Continuing to work with you, even at a higher cost, is the road of least resistance.

On the other hand, bear in mind that the client might have their own topline in terms of their willingness to pay, and you may have just broken through it. If so, remember what we covered in chapter 2: you only want to work for the right clients, so if this one is no longer right for you, it's time to let them go. I have gone down this road several times in my freelance career, and I've never regretted it.

So conquer your fear of the unknown and raise your prices with confidence. Whatever happens, you will be OK.

57 Record what you charge

If you follow the advice I've given so far, you're likely to end up charging a range of different prices for different clients. That can make it hard to keep track of which ones might be due for an increase, or what your going rate should be for a particular type of project.

If you have a superb memory for figures, you may be able to hold it all in your head. Failing that, your invoices provide a reliable, if rather cumbersome, record of your past actions. But I think it's far better to keep a concise, at-a-glance record of what you've charged to whom.

To do that, just create a simple spreadsheet or table showing the client, the project and what you charged for it. Alongside, record any notes about how the project went – particularly details about how accurate your price was. For example, 'took longer than expected', 'loads of changes and revisions' and so on. These sorts of comments are pointers to prices that you *definitely* need to increase next time around.

Even if you use project rates exclusively, your spreadsheet could still include some quantity or time ratios for your private use. For example, you could see how your price per word would stack up across a range of articles of various lengths, or what nominal hourly rate you're getting across different types of photoshoot. This could help you keep your prices consistent or highlight discrepancies between clients.

You can use your record both to tweak project prices within the same general pricing framework, and also to impose an across-the-board increase when you feel the time is right. This is particularly useful when you do a lot of work for the same client, and you want to make sure you're being consistent about price. Work through your list and apply a consistent markup to each one to arrive at the new price for each project type.

In my experience, most clients probably won't be analyzing your prices in the same depth as you are. For larger organizations in particular, pretty much *any* freelancer's price is small potatoes in comparison to their other suppliers' costs – a point that's worth remembering when you're contemplating an increase. So they will probably just plug your project price into their own budget, and as long as the numbers still work, that will be enough. They will only query a price if it 'seems high' to them, whatever 'high' means in context.

Whatever your clients do, though, it helps to have historical pricing information at your fingertips, so you can keep your pricing approach internally consistent and be ready with a credible response if you are questioned. It's also good for your own peace of mind and self-esteem to know that you're being professional about your prices – not just shooting from the hip or trying your luck, and running the risk of being caught out.

58 Push past your own precedents

In chapter 3, we saw how precedents can be powerful. They lock your prices in at a profitable level, allowing you to replicate good deals over and over again.

So far, so good. However, when it comes to increasing your prices, those same precedents can be a double-edged sword. With the passage of time – say, three or four years – the old price may start to lag behind what you now charge new clients. But in your mind, it's still 'a good price', making you reluctant to revisit it. Your satisfaction at having originally struck the deal lingers on, making that client/price combination somehow sacred in your mind.

Therefore, you may have to make a conscious effort to overcome the precedents that you yourself have set. Instead of regarding them as achievements you want to preserve, you have to switch over to seeing them as foundations that you can build on – or even problems you need to fix.

That's not to say you need to take a pushy or aggressive tone with your client. Whatever you're charging them is your responsibility, not theirs. You just need to find a tactful way to open a conversation with them about a raise.

If you record what you charge (see above), that makes it easy to see how long your current pricing regime has been in place. If you're anything like me, it will be longer than you thought. In fact, you can use your findings to build your case for a raise – for example, by saying something like 'My prices have been at the same level since 2019.'

By pointing this out, you're implying that you've been holding prices down to stay competitive – even though it was probably just inertia or forgetfulness on your part. You also highlight that you haven't made any increases at all for inflation, which constitutes a reduction in real terms. But even if the client isn't sensitive to all this, they still have to acknowledge that several years without an increase has been a good deal for them, and that it's time to give something back. And if they don't acknowledge it – well, the price is going up regardless.

59 Keep up with inflation

One way to get a sobering perspective on price rises is to consult an online inflation calculator. Enter the rate you charge a client, and the year when you started them off on that rate. Now see how much that rate *should* be today, just to give you the same buying power. You may be surprised.

I once did this when I was planning to jack up the daily rate for a longstanding client by about 30%. When I fed in the old rate – which I'd stupidly left unchanged for around a decade – I was dismayed to discover that most of my so-called 'big increase' had already been eaten up by inflation, and I'd only be making about £20 per day extra. I thought I was cashing in, but in reality I was catching up.

On the plus side, inflation is a pretty watertight rationale for increasing your prices. But as this story shows, it's also why you need to keep on top of your prices and increase them regularly. Set a reminder to do it once a year, or tie it in with another annual task, like your tax return. Otherwise, you're effectively giving clients a progressively *lower* rate year on year. Then, you end up hitting them with a rise that *looks* huge, but is actually just bringing you in line with the cost of living.

60 Double your prices (or just think about it)

So, just how ambitious could you be about price increases? Well, some people advocate simply doubling your prices.

That's right. Double them, just like that. Starting from tomorrow morning, you quote twice what you're charging today. Just imagine!

Now, the very idea of this strikes fear into the heart of many freelancers. Quite naturally, they imagine losing loads of their clients at a stroke. When you've painstakingly built up your precious client base over many years, carefully cultivating a relationship with each individual client, making a big price rise across the board feels like unleashing a bull in a china shop.

Nobody really wants to 'fire' multiple clients in one go – not least because of the emotional turmoil involved. However, from a purely financial perspective, doubling your prices could make sense. After all, if you double your prices and lose half your clients, you're earning the same money in half the time. In the other half, you can earn more money or just have fun. It's easy to see how this brings you a *lot* closer to your wealth goals.

What's more, doubling your prices will have a knock-on effect in other areas – like the way prospects perceive your service. Immediately, you're putting yourself on a level with a whole new set of competitors, and inviting prospects to compare you with them, like for like. Just as a lower price makes your service look average, so a higher one makes it look premium. All else being equal, we expect more expensive items to be higher-quality. So in a sense, your higher prices may sell themselves.

Now, you might be thinking you can't actually live up to those higher expectations. But what if your premium prices affect *your* perceptions too, so you 'bootstrap' yourself up to a whole new level of achievement? By 'acting as if' you're a top-flight provider (see chapter 5), you might give yourself the impetus to actually become one.

Having said all that, big increases do bring some risk. If you get it wrong, you could price yourself right out of the market – or at least miss out on some jobs or clients you really want.

Or, even if your increase does work out, you might still become dependent on a handful of clients who are willing to pay top dollar. That could make your income more precarious, in the sense of having more eggs in fewer baskets. So ironically, price-doubling might work best if you *already* have a big financial cushion as insurance (see chapter 2).

In the end, 'double your prices' might be more of a thought experiment than a viable strategy. When you imagine doing it, you get back in touch with your power. You remember that the fate of your business is in your hands, and that you can always choose to make big, bold changes.

OK, maybe you can't double your rates. But how about charging half as much again? When you've seriously thought through the implications of a 100% jump, adding on 50% doesn't seem so radical. (This is an example of anchoring, which we saw in chapter 5 – but this time, the technique works on you rather than your prospect.)

Exploring these possibilities also reminds you of *why* you're putting your prices up in the first place. It's not just to 'get more money', but to strike the right balance between clients, workload, earnings and time. Contemplating big increases helps you weigh up what you might be willing to risk in one area in order to make a gain in another. Even if doubling your prices isn't right for you, you can use it to discover the pricing strategy that is.

61 Increase your earnings target

In chapter 2, we looked at setting a target for your annual earnings. At the end of each year, you'll need to review your progress against that target, and decide what to do next:

- If you *missed your target by miles*, you may want to revise it downwards. If you get it into your head that your target is simply unachievable, it will lose its power to motivate you. In the worst case, you'll start resenting the targets you've set yourself, and become your very own boss from hell.

- If you *just missed your target*, you could keep it in place for the following year and have another try. You came close, but no cigar. Next time, you'll nail it for sure. Take a look at the shortfall, and think about how you could make it up – more clients, price increases, new services or whatever.

- If you *reached or beat your target*, you can step it up to a new, higher level and see if you can continue your upward momentum. Clearly, the sky's the limit!

However, I'd like to throw in a couple of caveats to this last point.

First, be honest with yourself about what it took to reach that target, and what it will take to go beyond it. Did you work flat-out the entire year to reach your goal? If so, is that level of effort actually sustainable – mentally, emotionally and physically? Reaching goals can be addictive – so don't let a fanatical obsession with targets for their own sake get in the way of your health, your relationships or your family.

If you can't keep working at the same intensity, that doesn't mean you have to abandon your new target. It just means you need to charge more rather than working more, as we saw earlier in this chapter.

Second, be sure you really *need* more money. Think back to the points we covered in chapter 1. What is true wealth for you? Why do you want money – and, more specifically, why do you want to make more money next year? Are you making more money for its own sake, when actually you're *already* in a position to enjoy the things you value most? (We'll come back to this theme towards the end of the book.)

Takeaways from this chapter

- To make more money without compromising on lifestyle or the quality of your work, increase your prices rather than your workload.

- Consider how to increase prices through both new and existing clients, and whether you should charge all your clients the same rate.

- Keep a record of what you charge, so you can easily see where and when to make increases.

- Consider every option for increasing prices, from simple inflation tracking and boosting your annual target right through to doubling your rates at a stroke.

- Revise annual targets upwards, but stay in touch with your personal goals, so you don't wind up chasing money for its own sake.

7 BEING BUSINESSLIKE

You may not have gone freelance to start a business, but you can still be businesslike in your freelancing. This chapter explores how you can develop the entrepreneurial side of your work by building new products, services and relationships.

62 Think business

One of the keys to freelance success is to think of your freelancing as a business – not just you, working away on your own.

You don't necessarily need to incorporate as a business. Some freelancers don't want the commitment, while others find that the costs and tax implications don't stack up. But if the numbers do add up for you, I would strongly advise you to form a company around your freelancing.

Starting your own company puts a formal separation between your personal and business finances. Then, you have a clear distinction between money that belongs to the business, and money that you've made a conscious decision to pay yourself.

I've found that this setup functions as an effective brake on my personal spending. If I want to buy something that's beyond the monthly salary I pay myself, I have to actually log into my business bank account and pay myself a dividend to cover it. That encourages me to retain earnings in the business and build up a financial cushion – which, as we saw in chapter 2, will give you a foundation to be more confident and ambitious about pricing.

However, being a company brings you psychological benefits too. It turns your freelance business into a 'thing' – a distinct commercial entity with its own identity and interests. Before, you were just a sole trader, but now you're the owner of a commercial concern. That motivates you to think about what's best for your business, as well as what's best for you.

Of course, they ultimately boil down to the same thing, since you are the sole proprietor and have absolute control. But when you think business, you naturally think in a more entrepreneurial, strategic way. Instead of just bringing in the cash, you're working to build long-term revenue streams that will help you realize your personal wealth goal. In other words, you're making strong progress towards the aims you identified in chapter 2.

That path might lead you to turn your business into a real corporation, with premises and employees. However, that's outside my own experience and beyond the scope of this book. So, in this chapter, we'll look at some ways you can be more businesslike within the format of a one-person business.

Unlike most of the other suggestions in this book, some of the ideas in this chapter are projects you can pursue rather than just principles to follow. Therefore, they involve some commitment in terms of energy and time. So in considering whether they might be right for you, be mindful of your personal circumstances.

For example, a tactic such as doubling your prices (chapter 6) involves practically no extra time or effort. It's a one-time decision that you take in your head, and put into practice from the next quote you send out. But things like branding yourself, developing service packages or taking up teaching (all covered in this chapter) might demand a much heavier commitment.

With that in mind, certain ideas might work better for you if you've reached a certain 'age and stage'. For example, if you're over 50 and no longer that interested in building up your freelance business any further, you could consider a combination of price increases, delegation and specialization, which could allow you to focus on the things you really enjoy, maintain your earnings and free up some of your time.

63 Brand yourself

People sometimes think of brands as being just logos or visual identities, but they're much more than that. In reality, a brand is the sum total of what people think about a company or organization. And it's these thoughts that allow it to charge a certain price for what it does.

The reason Apple can charge £1000 for a phone is not that it has a cool logo. It's because it has a longstanding reputation for products of a particular quality and style, which is *represented* by the Apple brand.

So do you, as a freelancer, need a brand?

Well, from the perspective I've just outlined, it's clear that *you already have one*. There are already some people, however few, who know about your freelance business. And they've already formed an impression, however vague, of what you're all about. People out there are having thoughts about your business, whether you like it or not.

So the real question is how *proactive* you're going to be about your brand. Are you going to just focus on your work, and let your brand take care of itself? Or are you going to put conscious thought and deliberate effort into developing your brand?

That's not meant to sound like an accusation. It's a genuine choice, and either approach can be valid. And for most freelancers, the right answer will be somewhere between these two extremes.

For example, few freelancers these days launch themselves into freelancing with no website, no social media, no public profile of any kind. To do that, you'd need to be confident that you could hustle up some work on ability alone – or that your network and reputation were already so strong that work would come to you.

But at the other extreme, you might not have the time, the resources or the inclination to create a multi-faceted, multi-channel brand for yourself, exploiting every possible branding avenue to the max. So instead, you'll want to choose the branding activities that make most sense for you – that is, that bring you a decent reward for a reasonable effort.

So, what sort of things are we talking about? Well, your branding activities could include some of the following:

- Writing a *profile or bio* to use on social-media sites, your own website and elsewhere. Actually, I would argue that every freelancer needs to do this, if only to clarify their own offer in their mind.

- Creating a *website* or online portfolio to promote your service. Again, this is probably essential, although some freelancers get by with profiles on social-media sites. A LinkedIn profile can certainly work as an online cv.

- Creating a *visual identity* for your business. As we've seen, a brand is more than just a logo. But having a logo gives people a visual 'hook' for all their thoughts about your freelance business, so you can build an identity that is consistent across channels and over time. Visual identities get a *lot* of exposure, so view this as a serious, long-term investment and don't be tempted to economize. Getting a cut-price visual identity is like buying a cheap suit for an interview.

- Choosing a ***trading name or business name*** that you can use in place of your own name. This immediately gives the impression of a larger, more professional outfit. It also allows you to send an early message to prospects about what you'll be like to work with – so choose your name with care.

- Writing a ***tagline*** that describes the unique value you offer, like 'The super-friendly sales trainer'. You can see many examples of individuals using these if you browse around some LinkedIn profiles.

- Creating a ***character or persona*** to represent you in public. Depending on your personality, you may already have done this to an extent, having developed a 'work you' that's perceptibly different from the 'real you'. With this approach, you deliberately cultivate a persona to express some aspect of your unique value. They could be an exaggerated or filtered version of yourself, or they could be radically different, like a cartoon character.

- ***Sharing your knowledge*** by writing or talking about your work or your industry in public forums. For example, you could write how-to guides, beginners' guides, FAQs, comment pieces, expert analyses or even books. All these are ways to *show* prospects the knowledge and attitude you bring to your work, as opposed to just telling them about it. You can also use longer pieces as lead magnets, where prospects enter their email address to access a download.

- *Sharing your work* by creating a portfolio of past projects and/or case studies. This is a good approach if you're uncomfortable with blowing your own trumpet and would prefer your work to speak on your behalf. Including client testimonials will add depth and dimension.

- *Getting yourself out there* by attending networking events or speaking at conferences. If you're naturally outgoing, this could work really well for you. You can build a strong network and spread the word about your service just by meeting people and chatting to them.

- *Using social media* to build a following, share your work, follow your industry and also get some valuable support from your fellow freelancers.

So, are these things going to bring in the business? Well, maybe not directly. Since a brand lives in people's thoughts, you carry out these activities to shape prospects' perceptions of you *before* they get in touch. In a sense, you're giving them the feeling of having worked with you, even if they haven't (yet). In financial terms, you're increasing the perceived value of your service, so you can charge more for it when the time comes.

Now, you might be thinking that it's all too much trouble. But you probably won't want to do *all* these things, all the time. Instead, you'll aim for a sensible *marketing mix*. In other words, you'll choose a set of marketing activities that is sustainable for you. That means you'll have enough time, energy and inclination to keep doing all your chosen tasks on a regular basis.

In choosing your marketing activities, you need to respect your own character. As noted above, things like sharing case studies or blogging are most likely to suit introverts, while networking and public speaking come more easily to extroverts.

I have found that making time for marketing activities is one of the toughest things about being a freelancer. You start with good intentions, probably when work is a little slow, and dutifully tick all the tasks off your list. It's easy to find the motivation, since you're short of work – and it's easy to find the time, for the same reason.

But then work picks up, and all that changes. Now, time is short, and your marketing jobs get pushed off the end of your to-do list. Plus, when your schedule is full, it's harder to generate the same sense of urgency. Do you *really* need to keep doing that stuff, now that work is so plentiful?

Try to keep going, however difficult it may be. Marketing is the generation of *future* cash flow. So your actions now don't relate to your current situation – they determine what's in store for you months or even years from today. You mend the roof while the sun is shining, not when raindrops start to fall.

Even if you're consistently busy, your branding still helps, by supporting those perceptions of a high-value service. Without them, all you have is supply and demand. In other words, people get in touch, and the price you give them is based purely on how busy you are. That might *imply* that you're pretty good, but it doesn't give any direct confirmation. With branding, you can establish value in your prospects' minds in a more constructive way.

64 Build service packages

As a freelancer, you're basically a butler for your clients. They can ask you to do pretty much whatever they want – add things in, change things round, try it a different way. In fact, there may be lots of times when you make a virtue of that, by saying you'll shape your approach around the client's needs.

To illustrate this point, B2B service providers often use the metaphor of off-the-peg suits vs. bespoke tailoring. (Confession: I've recycled the line 'nothing fits like a tailored suit' for several copywriting clients over the years.)

However, 'made to measure' has a downside: the prospect must know what they want. They must have enough understanding of their own needs, and your industry, to frame their own requirement. If they don't have this insight, you have to enlighten them. Otherwise, you can't really move forward, because your proposal and price will lack context.

Let's say you work with small business owners or startup founders. By definition, most of them are at the start of their learning journey, and there are many business services that they have never sourced before. Indeed, if they are first-time entrepreneurs, they may be completely new to the whole concept of outsourcing. And they may not even appreciate that they lack this knowledge.

If you ask a prospect like this what they want from, say, their website, or their office cleaning service, they'll give you *some* sort of answer – but it won't necessarily be complete or accurate. So you risk leaving valuable business on the table, purely because your prospect didn't know they needed it. (Or, on the flip side, you might provide something they *thought* they needed, but actually didn't – which probably won't lead to repeat business.)

One way round this problem is to build service packages. Basically, you 'bundle' a number of tasks or deliverables together, and offer them for a fixed price. For example, a graphic designer could offer a startup business pack comprising designs for a logo, a leaflet and a business card, plus printing.

Clients like packages because they remove uncertainty. A package sends a strong message of 'This is right for you,' so clients feel more confident about buying.

Packages also show clients that you understand them, because you've already considered and anticipated their most likely needs. So a package sale might well lead to other, more customized work later on.

On your side, packages have a feeling of being solid and fixed that makes prospects less likely to question them. Unlike a tailored service, they do not come across as negotiable or flexible. The prospect either wants the package or they don't.

What's more, the price is baked in, so you don't have to consider it afresh with each new enquiry, and that saves you time on the quoting process. All you have to do is write some sales copy to describe the package, after which it can pretty much 'sell itself'.

An all-in-one package probably says 'economy' rather than 'premium', and clients who choose a package accept that they are trading flexibility for affordability. However, that doesn't necessarily mean you have to offer a major discount. You just want price and package together to give the *impression* of a good deal.

You might be able to achieve that by throwing in things that are relatively quick or easy for you, but still add a lot of value for the specific clients you'll be targeting.

For example, in chapter 3 we looked at the potential value of 'just having a look'. Maybe your package could comprise some solid hands-on tasks, plus a quick 'health check' or consultancy session that clients will find really useful.

Another option is to throw in learning materials, such as the beginners' guides or books we looked at in the previous section. Once you've developed these materials, it's no extra effort to include them – but the client might really appreciate them. If they're exclusive to the package, so much the better.

In developing your package, you'll want the various elements to reinforce each other and deliver a coherent value combination. For example, an SEO consultant could offer a link-building project (hands-on), a quick website health check ('having a look') and an ebook introducing clients to SEO (knowledge resource).

This is a great starter pack for SEO – yet it also primes the client to come back, because SEO is a long-term project, and they probably won't learn enough from the starter pack to take it on. So although this service package may seem to be teaching the client to do the work themselves, it's actually showing them why they should buy it from an expert.

On the flip side, watch out for offering 'introductory' packages that actually make more sense as standalones, and therefore won't lead to future work.

For example, a designer offering a startup business pack might be hoping to pick up all their clients' future design work. So they give their package a modest price tag on that basis. But in fact, the startup might not have any more design work for several years – if ever. The fish can eat the worm off the hook and just swim away.

To ensure your packages make financial sense on their own terms, ask yourself whether you'd be happy to be invoicing nothing else but multiple instances of this package, day in, day out. If the answer is 'no', you need to rethink the price tag.

65 Offer a package menu

Packages are great, but they're still a 'take it or leave it' proposition. To give your prospects more options, you can build multiple packages and offer a menu that they can choose from.

With this approach, the prospect has a choice of options, but they all mean working with you. (In neuro-linguistic programming, this is known as a 'double bind': a choice at one level where each option amounts to the same thing at a higher level.)

How you slice up your offering depends on your line of work:

- You can offer different levels of service within the same task – like 'bronze', 'silver' and 'gold'.
- If you offer several different services, you could create a package for each one.
- Or you might want to build specific packages for different types of client, so each group has an option explicitly targeted at them.

You can also combine these approaches. For example, the 'Starter SEO pack for small businesses' from the previous section is aimed at a certain level (beginner) *and* a certain client type (small firms).

One effective way to market your packages is to offer prospects a set of three parallel options. In visual terms, you can display them side by side – for example, on a leaflet or web page.

The one on the left is the cheap option, with relatively few elements (so you could call it 'economy', 'basic', 'starter' or 'entry-level'). The one in the middle offers a balance of cost and features ('regular', 'original' or 'classic'). And the one on the right is more expensive, and includes everything ('premium', 'pro' or 'enterprise').

Most people will shy away from the extremes and plump for the safer middle way. However, you'll still have to make sure the other two packages are viable. Specifically, don't offer a rock-bottom 'budget' option in the hope that it will encourage people to opt for 'regular'. Some clients will always go cheap – and, to be fair, they might want to try you out before they make a bigger commitment.

You can also nudge people towards particular options based on their own priorities or preferences. For example, the cheap option could be labelled 'most affordable' or 'best value', the premium option could be labelled 'most comprehensive' and the standard option could be labelled 'most popular'. This 'popular' positioning harnesses the power of social proof: when people are unsure what to do, they prefer to copy others, or to follow the herd.

The key to offering choice is balance. While having *some* options can make prospects more likely to buy, too much choice can throw them into option paralysis: the inability to choose because there are too many possibilities. That's why a choice of three clearly differentiated bundles may work really well, while 10 micro-variations of the same service might simply bamboozle your prospects.

The more packages you provide, the closer you are to circling back to a 'tailored' service, where the client simply tells you what they want. Even if that does end up happening, though, the packages still serve as a framework to educate the prospect and guide them towards thinking about options and prices in a realistic way. Some B2B firms embrace this, and are happy to offer an off-the-shelf product, a customized product or a tailored service, as the client prefers.

At the end of the day, what really matters is that you close the sale at the right price – not that you prove that your packages are viable, or railroad the client into buying in a particular way.

66 Work on retainer

With a retainer arrangement, you agree to work a set number of hours or days for the same client on a regular basis. For example, you might agree to do one day a week for a client, or three days a month.

The two main attractions of a retainer are predictable workload and consistent earnings. Once it's set up, you can just keep doing your contracted hours and getting paid. If you manage to put several retainer arrangements in place, you could lock in a guaranteed monthly income, combining the freedom of freelancing with the security of a salary.

However, that commitment cuts both ways. When you sign a retainer, you're selling your future availability. Once you've agreed the retainer, you can't easily walk away from it just because a higher-paying client or a more attractive project turns up. So in this sense, retainers can impose an upper ceiling on your earnings, as well as giving them a lower floor.

Before you sign a retainer, carefully consider what tasks are involved, and what volume of work is available. You could be signing away your time without really knowing how you'll be spending it. And as we saw in chapter 5, it always pays to be cautious about 'lots of work in the pipeline'.

Even if the work you want is there, you may still become over-dependent on a single client. In my experience, many freelancers wind up in this position, with one or two clients accounting for a big proportion of their income. I guess you could argue that a retainer is just formalizing that arrangement, so at least you get the benefit of predictable work. But on the other hand, maybe you shouldn't be actively embracing a situation that could pose a risk.

Price negotiations enter the frame too. The client might ask for a bulk discount, and you might decide to accept a lower rate to close the retainer deal. But what if the client takes that lower rate as a precedent, and tries to extend it to other work? If you have become dependent on them, you might find it difficult to say no.

Also, what happens if you agree a discount, but there isn't enough work for you to do? You could wind up doing fewer hours at a discounted rate – fine for the client, but the worst of both worlds for you. Or you could have a simple disagreement over how long certain projects should take – a problem with all time-based arrangements, as we saw in chapter 3.

For all these reasons, you probably don't want to jump straight into a retainer deal with a completely new client. Try to divert them into a project-based arrangement instead – perhaps by slicing off a single project to do as a trial, as described in chapter 5.

Sometimes, clients will ask you to work your retainer time in-house, sitting alongside their own employees. I've done this myself, and I found it to be a double-edged sword.

On the plus side, the arrangement gave me a deep and lasting insight into my client's business, and I got to know everybody I worked with really well. But the problem was that I 'went native': I lost my outsider's perspective, which is a big part of the value that freelancers offer. Overall, I was pretty relieved when the retainer came to an end and I could go back to working on their projects because I was needed – not just because I was there.

Finally, note that there may also be unfavourable tax implications if you work regular hours in-house and could be considered to be a part-time employee of the firm. Check your local regulations before you agree to anything.[5]

---

[5] In the UK, this is covered by the IR35 legislation, which is designed to ensure that 'disguised' employment is taxed at the same level as regular employment. At the time of writing, the regulations are being revised.

Sell service subscriptions

I'm sure you're familiar with the concept of 'software as a service'. Instead of buying a software package for a one-off fee, you pay a regular subscription that entitles you to updates and support. The best-known example is probably Microsoft 365.

Service subscriptions take the same idea into the freelance world. Basically, you combine the best elements of a service package and a retainer deal, to offer your clients ongoing support in a particular area. For example:

- A digital marketing consultant could take care of her clients' social media feeds, creating regular posts and responding to queries on their behalf.

- A website developer could make sure his clients' sites were running smoothly, with the latest software and strong protection against spam and viruses.

- A personal trainer could offer a weekly training session, with monthly fitness assessments and an annual review of progress.

When you're on a time-based retainer, the client can ask you to do whatever they want. So there's a risk that the tasks they request won't play to your strengths, or deliver that much benefit. But when you're designing a service subscription yourself, you can make sure it adds value – not just each month, but over a longer timeframe too.

One way to demonstrate this added value is with regular checkups or reports. In addition to doing the hands-on work, you also give the client information on the progress you've made, and how it's helping their business. The more numbers and graphs you can include, the more solid your value will appear.

Hard data might also help you fend off sceptical bean-counters. With a time-based retainer, you'll be putting in a big invoice every month, but you may not be able to point to any completed projects to justify it. So the client's accountant might start asking what they're getting for their money.

This is particularly likely if you work in-house, and they can see you spending time in meetings. Of course, discussions add value for the client – but their financial director might not see it that way. With reports at your fingertips, you can make a solid case for the benefit your work is bringing to the client.

If you decide to offer a subscription, you'll need to take a similar approach as you do to pricing by the project: write down exactly what the client gets for their money, so there's no dispute later on.

68 Buddy up

Freelancing can be a lonely business. Sure, you may be able to outsource some support services, or chat to a sympathetic freelancer from time to time. But the big questions, like business and marketing strategy, are yours and yours alone. And if you're a natural extrovert, you have to get used to working through all these issues on your own.

Buddying up offers a partial solution to both problems. Basically, you partner with another freelancer to establish a shared vehicle for marketing your respective services. It's what big firms call a 'strategic alliance' or 'joint venture', but at an individual level.

Forming an alliance offers you the chance to market yourselves as a company, without necessarily being one. If you're currently trading under your own names, you can build a shared brand and project the image of a far larger, more professional organisation. That could unlock opportunities that would otherwise be out of reach.

The key points to consider are:

- *Who* are the partners? Will there be two, three or even more of you? Could others join later?
- What are your *aims*? Are you looking to build a self-supporting venture, drum up some new business or just hang out and shoot the breeze?
- Will you actually *form a company*, or just create a new brand, trading name or website to market the partnership on a less formal basis? (The former is stronger, but harder to unpick later on. The latter is simpler and easier, but less robust.)
- How will you *make decisions*? If people don't agree, how will you resolve the deadlock?
- How will you approach *business tasks*? Will you assign equal responsibility for each one, or share them out? For example, you'll probably want to discuss who will work on bringing in new business, to avoid recriminations later on.
- Who will do the *marketing*? How will they find the time and, if needed, the money?
- What *services* will you offer, and how will you describe them to prospects?
- How will you *collaborate on projects*? Will you work together on each project, offer complementary or coordinated services or allocate entire projects to one of the partners?
- How will you decide who gets to pursue *new opportunities* that come in? (For example, you could consider leads

generated through your alliance website as belonging to the partnership, and leads that come through your own sites as your own.)

- How will you *allocate time* to the alliance? Specifically, how will you prevent 'real work' from dragging you back to your respective freelance businesses? Or will you just accept that you'll work on the alliance whenever you have time?
- Are you equally *committed*? Being honest, how much of a priority is the alliance for each of you? Will that be a problem?
- How will you *share the rewards*? If there's no formal entity for the partnership, who will actually invoice, receive the money and pay it out?

Maybe that all sounds a bit heavy – particularly for something that's supposed to lighten your load. But it's important to clarify what you want up front, because things could get tricky later on if your expectations diverge. You don't want to lose a friendship for the sake of an alliance.

I have been involved in a collaboration like this. Based on my experience, I have to warn you that your freelance alliance may not set the world on fire. For instance, you may find that it remains peripheral to your main business, or that it doesn't last that long. However, it might still generate some valuable leads in the meantime, and it'll probably boost your image in ways that are difficult to detect. If nothing else, you'll get some company and some informal support. Plus you'll get the fun experience of pursuing a project that *you* control, and working with collaborators of your choosing, who you really like and respect.

With all this in mind, the most important thing about an alliance is that everyone has their eyes open at all times. Everyone knows the deal, everyone is committed and everyone gets fair reward. As soon as an alliance no longer meets that test, it's time to rethink it – or just let it naturally fade away.

69 Delegate

When you delegate, you pass a task to a supplier so that you can concentrate on other things. It might be a task that you could easily have done yourself, or it could be something that your supplier can actually do better or quicker than you ever could – like your accounts.

Delegation can maximize the time you spend on high-earning activities. At the same time, you may be able to make a margin on work that other people do (that is, you charge your client more for that task than you pay to your supplier).

However, delegation has psychological benefits too. The feeling that other people are supporting you gives you a sense of strength and forward momentum. And because you're no longer responsible for absolutely everything, you also gain a sort of mental breathing space, which you can use to think more expansively about how your business could develop.

In today's connected economy, your supplier can be literally anywhere in the world. So you can benefit from the lower labour costs of a developing country. You can also reap some time-zone benefits – for example, if you're in the UK and delegate work to India, you may be able to get it done overnight. This could translate into a selling point for your own service.

Delegation might be familiar to you from salaried roles you've held. For example, if you previously managed a team, or had an assistant, you already know how to pass tasks on to others. And many of us get paid help with domestic tasks such as window cleaning or decorating.

Nevertheless, some freelancers get it into their heads that their business should only consist of themselves doing all the work. This can happen if their freelance role is similar to a previous hands-on job, and they never break free of their old job description, or the 'time for money' exchange of a salaried role.

Other freelancers simply aren't comfortable with the idea of employing other people, or playing the role of a boss. They don't like tasks like setting prices, requesting changes or chasing up late work, which can put them in the position of imposing their authority or even resolving disputes.

If you feel this way, delegation may not be for you. However, this mindset is very similar to the one I described in chapter 1, where freelancers shy away from money mind because they feel it clashes with their character. Refusing to contemplate delegation can hold you back in a very similar way, because it keeps you stuck in a cycle of endless busywork that restricts your opportunities to develop your freelance business.

So, how can delegation work in a freelance setting? Let's break down some of your options.

You can get help with...

- *Supporting tasks and admin.* For example, a virtual assistant could help by answering phone calls or chasing invoices. You get more time to spend on 'real work', and benefit from someone else's watchful eye on the formal side of your business.

- *Business development.* Some assistants will take on marketing tasks such as running your social media, sending out marketing material or even cold-calling prospects on your behalf. You can avoid tasks you really dislike, plus having someone else involved could keep you from slacking, so your marketing plan stays on track.

- *Specialized or expert tasks*. Some areas, like accounting and law, are clearly best left to professionals. But there might be grey areas where you have a choice over whether to learn a skill yourself or just delegate it. For example, a designer might pass complex Photoshop editing over to a specialist. By delegating, you save yourself the time and trouble you would otherwise have to spend learning the skill.

- *Repetitive or lower-value parts of your work*. For example, if you make corporate videos, there might be simple video editing tasks that someone else could do, while you focus on higher-level tasks like sketching out storyboards and writing scripts.

- *Project work*. In other words, you could commission another freelancer, or even a company, to do some or all of the main hands-on work for a project. Ideally, you make a margin on the deal, while working on another paying project yourself.

With supporting tasks, your chosen provider must be reliable, knowledgeable and trustworthy enough to do what they promise. It's hard to get a sense of how profitable this type of delegation is, because you're dealing with an overhead rather than billable work. In other words, these are non-project tasks that nobody really pays for – they just take up your time. So you just need to be sure that you're always gaining time on the deal, not losing it.

With actual project work, you need to be a little more analytical. Obviously, you want to make money on the deal – but the calculation isn't quite as simple as it sounds.

Let's say you're a writer, like me. Your cunning plan is to delegate the drafting of an article to a less experienced freelancer who is keen as mustard and hungry for work. You've quoted £200 to the client, and you reckon you can get the junior writer to do it for £75. That's a sweet £125 heading straight into your pocket for doing absolutely nothing.

Except it's not.

First, you need to actually find your junior. That means combing through resumes and portfolios to identify someone with the right skills. Then, they need to be available and contactable – neither of which are guaranteed with freelancers (of any age).

Having chosen your supplier, you'll have to brief them on the client and the job. That could easily take an hour or two, whether you do it in writing or in a call. But even then, you could still be dealing with their questions throughout the job.

Then, when you get their work back, you'll need to check it thoroughly. What if your supplier has plagiarized some text? How many sources did they use? Did they even do it themselves, or farm it out again, to someone even cheaper?

Since the client is dealing with you, any problems with the work are on your head. No matter how small the job, your professional reputation is still on the line. At the end of the day, you can outsource the task, but not the risk.

Then, when the client comes back with changes, you need to review them and pass them back to your junior, with an explanation, for them to handle. But then you'll have to check their work *again* – so you might decide that it's easier just to do the amendments yourself. Either way, you're putting in yet more time, and your profit margin is melting away before your eyes.

As this story shows, the choice of subcontractor is crucial. A reliable one is gold, while a flaky one can make the whole thing a waste of time.

What's more, communication can be just as important as hands-on ability – perhaps even more so. Seeing eye to eye makes the difference between delegation that runs like clockwork and a disorganized mess.

The better the provider, the more experienced – and expensive – they're likely to be. So you can see how hard it is to delegate higher-value tasks to others and still make money on the deal. If they know their own value, they'll probably be pricing near your topline already (chapter 5). There may not be enough of the pie left over for you to get a decent slice.

If you're hesitating over whether or not to delegate project work, get back in touch with your unique value, which we saw in chapter 3. Clients are probably not hiring you as a pure project manager; they're hiring you for your hands-on skills. So think carefully before you outsource stuff that they probably have a right to expect from you. As a simple test, ask yourself how they'd feel if you revealed that you'd delegated this task. As long as they wouldn't mind, you're good to go.

70 Specialize

Imagine you have a precious piece of furniture, maybe an heirloom, that you want to have restored. Your regular handyman says he's happy to do it for £100. But you also speak to a specialist furniture restorer. She explains the techniques and materials she'll use in detail, then quotes a price of £450. Who will you choose?

As this illustration shows, specialists have strong appeal for clients who have particular needs. They promise higher quality and lower risk. And because they're harder to find in the market, they can also charge more.

When you specialize, you narrow down your service in order to make it more appealing to a certain subset of clients. There are a number of ways to do this:

- *Service specialization*, where you offer a specific service or type of work (for example, designing annual reports instead of general graphic design)
- *Client specialization*, where you focus on a particular client group (for example, startup food businesses instead of firms of any type)
- *Need specialization*, where you focus on meeting a particular need, or helping clients in a certain situation (for example, first-time homebuyers, or firms facing a public-relations crisis)
- *Geographical specialization*, where you focus on serving clients in a certain area.

You can also combine different types of specialization – for example, by offering personal training to professionals within a 30-mile radius of your home.

When you specialize, prospects within your target group may feel a powerful pull towards your service, because it speaks to them so directly. And the narrower your niche, the more powerful the pull.

Depending on what you do, you may be one of just a few freelancers to offer your speciality – perhaps even the only one. If so, the prospect may already see you as special and desirable, purely because you are so rare.

On a project level, the prospect knows that you will probably have a good understanding of their needs, because you've dealt with similar clients before. That saves time and reduces risk for them. They also expect a more thoughtful, nuanced and sophisticated service, because you spend your *whole time* thinking about projects like theirs.

Depending on the type of clients you serve, you may find that you get word-of-mouth referrals within your target group, which is hugely valuable. Or there may be specialist communities that you can target – for example, by advertising through trade associations or industry-specific magazines and websites. Writing articles and posts that display your specialist knowledge is another excellent way to promote your niche service.

Specializations are great for search engine marketing, because you can target search terms that are less popular, and therefore may be easier or cheaper to rank higher for. These are known as 'long tail' terms. For example, while there are currently 55.2m Google results for 'copywriter', the results for 'annual report copywriter' number 1.1m. If you can capture that traffic, you've eliminated 98% of your competition at a stroke.

However, specializing also involves trade-offs. By definition, the tighter your focus, the fewer potential clients you have. So you need to be sure of two things: first, that there are enough clients in your target group to keep you in work, and, more to the point, that you can actually reach and serve them effectively. For example, your osteopathy service for the over-70s may be world-class, but how many seniors are living in your local area? And are you sure they'll be online and searching for your website?

Finally, remember why you're reading this book. As we saw in chapter 2, your clients need to reach the BAR – that is, they benefit and appreciate your service *and* have enough resources to pay for it. Everyone wants good relationships with their clients, but a cosy love-in with your niche targets isn't necessarily going to help you get paid. For example, you may offer a superb careers counselling service for 20-somethings – but people at the start of their careers aren't usually flush with cash. With the best will in the world, you're running a business, not a charity.

71 Semi-specialize

By 'semi-specialize', I mean that you add a specialization to your service portfolio – but you don't necessarily call it that, or consciously develop it, or drop any of your other services to narrow your focus.

Let me give you an example from my own career. Soon after I went freelance, I was offered some academic editing work by an existing contact. Although it wasn't really my skillset, I was happy to do it, and the client kindly referred me on to their colleagues. Since academics have many contacts at other institutions, and also tend to move around themselves, I eventually wound up with an international network of academic clients.

However, I don't have any formal training or qualifications for this line of work, and I've never consciously tried to develop it. So while this has become a really important area of business for me, and is arguably a specialist skill, I still don't really promote it as a specialization. And since I still do plenty of general writing work alongside it, I'm not really specializing, as such.

So, if I didn't do anything proactive, what's the lesson for you? I think it's to remain open to every opportunity, even if it's outside your core skillset, whatever you consider it to be. Don't let what you 'should' do limit what you *could* do. If a new specialization starts to grow naturally – and it pays – then just follow wherever it leads. You don't need permission.

This applies even if you've already decided to specialize in a different area. If one specialization worked well for you, why not two, or even more? Nobody's counting – and besides, there are no rules.

Business scholars call this sort of approach *emergent strategy*.[6] Instead of creating a master plan and trying to impose your will at every turn, you let your strategy emerge naturally as your intentions interact with events. Over time, your freelance business 'becomes itself' as the path through the forest becomes clear.

If you take this approach, stay flexible about the way you describe yourself and your services. You don't have to mention everything you do to everybody; you can be different things to different people. Although I have a brief page about academic editing on my website, all the important detail is in the longer information sheet I described in chapter 4. And since the work mostly comes through word of mouth, there's no need for me to publicize it too heavily.

72 Generalize

Having looked at specialization, we should also take a look at the opposite strategy: generalization.

As a generalist, you don't focus on any one area in particular. You simply position yourself as a generic service provider, and give yourself a 'job title' to match – for example, a web designer, a photographer, a copywriter.

The downside of this approach is that you miss out on the benefits of specialization. You won't have a particularly strong appeal to certain client types, or people with certain sorts of projects. Instead, you'll have broad appeal to everyone. That might make it harder to market yourself, because you might end up blending in with the rest of your market. In marketing-speak, you lack differentiation.

---

[6] Henry Mintzberg, *The rise and fall of strategic planning: Reconceiving roles for planning, plans, planners* (Free Press, Toronto, 1994).

However, there are many compensations once you're actually working with clients. You could become their 'go-to guy', who they trust to handle many different types of work. Then you can build a strong, long-lasting relationship with them and make valuable contributions across many areas. After a while, you become indispensable.

A deeper relationship brings deeper learning. When you do all sorts of work for a client, you get to know them (or their business) back to front. You may also end up working with several different people within their organization. That sort of closeness makes it far quicker and easier for you to get up to speed with their new projects. You may even be able to suggest some ideas of your own.

Once you have your feet under the table, you're hard to dislodge. As you've probably discovered already, trust and reliability are like gold dust in the freelance world. Even if clients find themselves with a specialized requirement, many would rather use someone they already know and trust than go back to the market for an expert. My clients have asked me to do things I've never done before – even over my own objections – purely because I've become their go-to copywriter.

That sort of situation is a win-win, because you can expand your service into new areas with far less risk than normal. In the normal course of events, you'd probably have to learn a new skill at your own expense, then put it into practice on your very first job for a new client. But this way, you get to learn on the job, get paid for it and enjoy a relaxed, trusting relationship throughout.

73 Diversify

Going one step beyond generalizing, you can diversify by deliberately adding more skills and services to your offer. This can bring more value to your clients, and unlock new earnings opportunities too.

Sometimes, new skills are forced on you by developments in your industry. For copywriters like me, the classic example is search engine optimization (SEO), which went from being a dark and unknown art to a must-have skill for anyone who wanted to write for the web. Being more proactive, you might spot some new opportunities that you could take by expanding your skillset. Or you might just want to learn new skills for yourself, so you can go in a direction you personally find interesting or appealing.

The rationale for diversification is that you get more fingers in more pies. You do more things, so you can target more clients and make more money. You can become a member of more specialized communities and build a wider network.

When it comes to diversifying, the crucial question is whether your various services *complement* each other.

Your services are complementary if they do one or more of these things:

- They draw on the same **skills**
- They appeal to the same **types of clients**
- They offer **related benefits or functions** – that is, they allow clients to do or achieve similar things
- They're **linked in clients' minds**, or they naturally **lead on to each other** somehow
- They can easily be **sold or marketed together**.

The more complementary your new service is, the easier it will be for you to add it. Ideally, your different services will support each other in a way that helps your freelance business to grow. For example, you might be able to cross-sell one service on the basis of another, or build a service package that includes both. Clients then get the benefit of a 'one-stop shop', which reduces their effort in terms of finding different suppliers and also the risk involved in co-ordinating everybody's work. Everything's simpler when you only have one number to call.

On the other hand, your new service might be something very different from what you do now – not so much a synergy as a side hustle. Indeed, you might take it on precisely so you can add more variety to your working life, and become more than a one-trick pony. On a commercial level, it might function as a hedge against market volatility: if your main business is going through a slack period, maybe your side hustle will fill in.

The danger with any diversification is that the further away the new service is from what you do now, the harder it will be to integrate it into your existing offering. There's a risk of spreading yourself too thin. You split your energies in too many different directions and end up being *less* than the sum of your parts, instead of more. This isn't just a problem for freelancers – even major multinationals who acquire firms in other areas often struggle to integrate them.[7]

For you, it may work fine in terms of day-to-day work. You can divide up your time and switch from one job to another without too much trouble. This gives you a nice sense of holding two jobs, both of which are interesting and lucrative for you. It's almost like you've been given another life to lead.

But what about marketing? For example, will you try to talk about everything you do on one website, or would that look a bit odd? Will you build two websites – or just accept that one or more services won't be featured at all?

---

[7] Some research suggests that as many as nine out of 10 mergers and acquisitions fail. See 'Why do up to 90% of Mergers and Acquisitions Fail?' by Annifer Jackson, *Business Chief*, 28 January 2020.

In the worst case, you could end up with a rag-bag of unrelated services that don't really make sense when you put them together – and that could put clients off using *any* of them. This is the fate that can befall freelancers who are simply good at lots of different things, or who have had patchwork careers. Through no fault of their own, their résumés or service portfolios end up looking a bit random – even though they may be very skilled at everything they do.

So, however you decide to diversify, you need to be able to market all your different skills at the right level. You also need to be able to persuade clients that your services make sense together, so you don't end up becoming a 'jack of all trades, master of none'.

Thinking about marketing also throws up another chicken-and-egg dilemma with diversification: you can only get into a new service by marketing it, but you might feel that you can't really market it until you've actually done it.

Some freelancers advocate simply claiming you've done something before, even if you haven't. The main objection to that is obvious: it's dishonest. But assuming that you have no problem with it ethically, could it actually work?

It's true that clients can never know for sure what you've done before, unless they request a reference direct from a previous client. You could claim to have done all sorts of stuff and say that you can't talk about it because of client confidentiality.

Even so, I'd find it hard to handle direct questioning about a service I'd never done. Maybe I could get away with saying, 'I've done it, but I can't discuss it.' But I think I'd still get found out when we got down to the nuts and bolts of the project. I'd never be able make my ideas and advice sound convincing. And if the client came back with negative feedback on my work, I'd be wondering why on earth I'd put myself in that position in the first place.

So, if you want to 'bootstrap' yourself into a new service, I suggest you walk as close to this line as you can, but without stepping over it. You can discuss the service on social media as much as you like – for example, by analyzing or reviewing what other people have done. You can talk about similar things you've done, and how they relate to this service. But I don't think you should make any false claims about your experience.

Look at it this way: if I was subcontracting to another freelancer, I wouldn't expect them to falsify their experience to gain the work. And I deal with my own clients on the same basis.

Now, there is another way to wriggle your way into a new service: doing free work in the area you want to target. Obviously, it's not a road to riches in the short term. But if working for free allows you to add a lucrative new string to your bow, it could be worthwhile. As well as brushing up your skills, you could get an insight into how the service will fit into your business – how much time it will take, what working process you could use and, of course, how much you could charge for it.

To make this sort of arrangement work, you just need to make sure both parties know and understand the deal. Since you will probably be the one making the approach, it's up to you to make everything clear at the outset.

For example, you could contact a local charity and say something like this:

> *I've never done a corporate video before, but I do have experience of video editing and volunteering, and I'd love to create a video for you. I won't charge you anything, and you don't have to use the finished piece. However, if you do use it, you agree to credit me in the video and let me*

promote it on my website and social media, without limitation. And if you don't use it, you'll allow me to anonymize it, by removing all your branding, and use it in my portfolio as a sample of my work.

This could then form the basis of a contract or letter of agreement between you to carry out the work.

As this example shows, free work is a sweet deal for the client in financial terms. But there could still be risks for them, which you may need to consider and address. By using a novice, they may be putting their reputation on the line, in which case they'll appreciate having the option to back out. And if the project is urgent, they won't want to wind up in a situation where they have to ask someone else to redo your work.

74 Teach

Do people want to know what you know? If so, you could earn money by teaching your skills to others.

Many freelancers these days share their knowledge one way or another. For example, every time you write a LinkedIn post about your work or industry, you're sharing what you know. You might put considerable effort into that writing, because it represents your skills and expertise in a public forum – but you still don't actually get paid directly for your effort. With teaching, you channel your energies towards developing paid-for products and services instead.

Teaching can generate revenue in itself, but it has the important side-effect of positioning you as an expert. After all, if you're teaching others, it follows that you must know the topic yourself. As a recognized authority in your field, you can charge more for your regular client work.

Here are some of the ways you can turn your knowledge into cash:

- *One-on-one training or coaching sessions* (in-person or virtual, through Skype, Zoom or Microsoft Teams)
- *Group training sessions* or *seminars* (again, either in-person or virtual)
- *Paid-for online courses* sold via platforms such as Teachable, Udemy, LinkedIn Learning and so on
- *Books and ebooks* published through self-publishing outlets such as Kindle Direct Publishing, Lulu, Unbound and so on.

In-person teaching could bring you a secondary revenue stream that could be a nice complement to your client work. If you're naturally outgoing, and get lonely when you're stuck in your office or workshop all day, this could be ideal for you.

On the other hand, options such as online courses and books hold out the promise of passive income, and may appeal more strongly to introverts. Your stuff can sit there online, selling steadily, without you having to do anything. While you may not make a life-changing amount of money, it could still be a very welcome top-up to your main work, or a boost for your financial cushion. Crucially, passive income keeps rolling in even if you go on holiday, take time off for sickness or even retire.

Whichever method you use, understand that it's going to take some work. With teaching, the barriers to entry are relatively high, because you need to develop *all* your teaching content before you give any lessons.

For example, seminars depend on preparation, presentations and handouts. Online courses need engaging video scripts and valuable downloads. And books take an astonishing amount of time to write and publish (or at least, the better ones do). If you're looking for a more casual, less labour-intensive way to start teaching, consider mini consultancy sessions (covered later in this chapter).

What's more, while some of these options offer potentially unlimited rewards, those rewards are also inherently uncertain. In contrast to the simple 'time for money' exchange of your client work, here you'll be investing your time with no guarantee of a return.

To reduce that risk, think about the business side before you start. Who will your students be? What will you teach them? And why will they choose you specifically? By answering these questions, you can find a way to transfer your unique value into the classroom, so your teaching stands out from the crowd and also works in harmony with your client work.

Even if you're sure of your unique value as a freelancer, you might still worry that your teaching won't really bring anything new or different to the party. With so much material now available online, it's easy to get discouraged about sharing what you know. Won't you just be repeating the same things that others have said before?

My answer to this is that while some ideas and information may indeed be out there already, your individual perspective on them is not. By expressing your knowledge in your own way, you will recreate and refresh it for a whole new audience. Your own identity, personality and experience will make your teaching unique, just as they do for your freelance service.

This is particularly true for women, people with disabilities, people of colour, LGBT people and anyone else whose voice is rarely heard in our culture. There are many people out there who would *love* to hear your truth about this stuff – if only because they're tired of straight, middle-aged white men being the gatekeepers of knowledge. *You* are the message – so let people hear it.

Some freelancers worry that by teaching their clients their own skills, they might do themselves out of a job. Personally, I don't think they will. While a client may be able to take on some simple tasks based on your teaching, they won't suddenly become you, or magically acquire your years of experience. In fact, once they have a go themselves, they may discover a newfound appreciation for the skills you bring to the table – making them more likely to use you, and less likely to question your price. So your teaching is actually more likely to function as a lead magnet for your regular business, rather than undermining it.

How soon can you start teaching? Well, over my career, I've been startled by the speed at which some freelancers move from learning their skills, to using them, and then on to teaching them. I turn around, and people I still think of as newbies are already offering online courses. And those courses are selling.

Of course, you don't necessarily need to know *everything* about a topic to teach it. You just have to know enough to teach your students what they need to know to reach a particular level of learning. So, if teaching appeals to you, and you think you could offer a pretty good beginner's guide to your area, don't wait. Do it now.

75 Move along the value chain

A value chain is a sequence of activities that add value to a product or service. Each stage in the chain adds a different type of value. The stages might all be done by the same organization, or by different organizations specializing at each stage.

For example, think about the value chain of manufacturing a smartphone. At the earliest stages, materials like metal and silicone are extracted from the earth. Then they're made into various components – the case, the screen and so on. Finally, the components are brought together to make the phone itself.

Generally, the further along the value chain you are, the more power you have. Instead of doing hands-on work, you add value by coordinating the work of other people, or by generating valuable ideas and intellectual property. Apple's most valuable asset is not its phone factory – it doesn't even have one – but its brand and product designs.

Sometimes, value chains expand and evolve as new stages emerge. The digital marketing industry is a good example.

In the early days of the 'world wide web', freelancers calling themselves 'web designers' could build websites single-handed. Then, as web technology became more sophisticated, getting one person to do everything was no longer viable – or desirable. Specialist web designers and web developers emerged: designers for the outward look and feel, and developers for the code that lay behind it. As technology and the expectations of website visitors evolved, so skills in both these areas had to advance.

Nowadays, we have digital consultants and agencies who simply coordinate all the other people involved in digital marketing. Even though they may do no hands-on work at all, they are still hugely valuable to their clients, who would otherwise have to navigate the complex and confusing digital landscape themselves.

What does all this have to do with freelancing? Well, there may be opportunities in your industry to become more strategic and less operational. In other words, to work more with ideas and processes, and less with tangible deliverables and hands-on tasks. The higher-level your service becomes, the more vital it is to clients – and the more you can charge for it.

How could you become strategic? Let's look at a few examples:

- Instead of editing fiction directly, you could offer expert feedback or criticism to authors.
- Instead of running firms' social media for them, you could simply advise them on how to set it up and manage it.
- Instead of designing websites, you could plan them out in order to improve users' experience.
- Instead of writing advertisements, you could develop a brand's tone of voice, which governs everything written for the brand.
- Instead of installing wiring into people's homes, you could advise them on where best to place power and data connections for their lifestyles and the characteristics of their property.

I'm saying 'instead of', but it could be 'as well as'. In other words, you could add the more strategic service on top of your existing offering, and offer them both, either separately or as an integrated package. Naturally, the strategic service will have a premium price tag.

Offering strategic advice fits well with some of the other ideas in this chapter. For example, as you become more strategic, it might make sense to delegate some hands-on tasks, so you can keep control over them as you move to a co-ordinating role. Or you might find that your strategic perspective naturally leads into a teaching role, as you explain to others how different services work or fit together.

76 Offer mini consultancy sessions

Suppose a client gets in touch and really likes your service, but they just can't afford you right now. You don't want to turn them away, but you also know you can't meet their expectations on price. What could you do?

We saw in chapter 3 how you should charge for thinking and talking, as well as doing. And we've just seen how teaching and moving up the value chain can be lucrative. Mini consultancy sessions offer a way to bring these ideas together in a low-risk, high-return way.

Basically, you offer a fixed period of consultancy for a fixed price. The client hires your brain by the hour, and gets the full benefit of your knowledge and experience – but *only* within this clearly bounded format.

You can offer your consultancy in person, on the phone or over a software platform such as Skype, Microsoft Teams or Zoom. Using a digital platform might allow either you or the client to record the call, to make a permanent record of it. Alternatively, you could offer to provide the client with a brief note summarizing what you've discussed.

Time is an important factor – both when the session starts, and how long it lasts. You'll probably want to schedule it for a time when your energy (both physical and mental) is at its height. For me, the most productive time is the middle of the morning, while mid-afternoon is a real low point. And I don't believe *anyone* really likes to begin a meeting after 4pm.

The length of the session is up to you. Personally, I find that I can't really speak productively over the phone for longer than an hour. I just can't sit still and stay 100% focused on a screen or a voice for longer than that. It's different if you're meeting in a coffee shop and you can stand up to buy a cake, visit the bathroom and so on. Or you could schedule a working lunch.

If you're really enjoying the session, and there's still a lot to talk about, you might feel OK about letting it overrun. But this has to be at your discretion – not the client holding you captive against your will. You could set an alarm or timer to give a gentle reminder towards the end, to make it easier to call a halt.

Ask your client to prepare a list of points they'd like to cover during the session, and review it in advance to make sure it's realistic. You don't want them to feel they've been short-changed if you don't cover everything on their list. For your part, you may need to keep the conversation focused, so you don't run out of time.

One issue to consider is how much preparation you'll do beforehand. For example, if you're a fiction editor, a writer might ask you to read their book, or part of it, before you provide feedback during a call. That all takes time, so if your sessions include this sort of prep work, make sure the price reflects it.

You may want to draw a distinction between *talking* about what you do and actually *doing* it. Will your words form a usable output for the client, or just guidance on how they can obtain one? Do you need to make that clear?

For example, if you pay me for my time, I will happily chat about different directions I could take with a copywriting job. I might even throw in a couple of headline ideas, if they pop into my head right there and then. But that's very different from creating my best and final draft, which I would be happy for you to take away and use. If you want that, I will have to go away and write it properly.

Mini consultancy sessions are a win-win. If an hour is all the client needs, that's great. You just made £150 (or whatever) for sitting and chatting over coffee. If they then decide that they actually want to use you more extensively, that's great too – you got paid for the hour, and now you've scored some work into the bargain.

Takeaways from this chapter

- Think of your freelancing as a business. It will give you the right mindset for developing it and maximizing your earnings.

- Working with others can be productive, either as an alliance of equals or as a way to delegate certain tasks.

- Decide whether you want to specialize, semi-specialize or generalize.

- Teaching others is an alternative way to get value from your skills.

- By becoming more strategic, you could offer more value while doing less hands-on work.

8 HOW MUCH IS ENOUGH?

It's fine to work hard for a better freelance life. Just don't keep striving for more if what you have is already enough.

Many thanks for reading this far.

Whether you've read the book from cover to cover, or just dipped into the parts that interested you, I hope you've found some helpful ideas among these pages.

I've shared as much of my knowledge as I can, but even so, this book is not the be-all and end-all of your freelancing fortunes. Not by a long chalk.

Instead, you should think of the ideas here as seeds. They can be a starting point to grow your own ideas, or unearth your own discoveries. I'm sure they'll take you to places I haven't even imagined.

Now, as we draw near to the end of the book, I'd like to circle back to some of the ideas from the very first chapter and look at them in a slightly different light. Specifically, I'd like to reflect on whether you can take your freelance freedom *too* far, and how much money is enough.

First, recall what it's like to be an employee. You don't get to choose what you do, who you work with, the hours you keep or how much you earn. Your employment can be snuffed out like a candle at any time, making you utterly dependent on the goodwill of your boss. Basically, you're living in a box.

However, those limitations have an upside. It's crystal clear what you have to do, and the package you'll receive in return. Unless you get promoted or change jobs, the road before you is straight and clear.

That clarity allows you to reflect on whether your position, and its rewards, are in line with your goals. OK, it's not perfect. But is it enough? Apart from some day-to-day gripes, is this job something you can settle for, given your age and situation? It's a simple question: yes or no.

Now contrast that with freelancing. As a freelancer, your working life is inherently messy and unpredictable. There's no fixed bundle of rewards on the table, no 360º appraisal, no annual pay rise. Freelancing is never truly finished; it's a *process* rather than a package.

The upside is that you're *always* free to try new things, act in new ways and make new connections – right up to the day you retire. But if you're always worrying that you still haven't 'arrived', your liberation can become a torment. Feeling perpetually unfulfilled, you descend into an endless quest for more and still more, until you don't even know why you want it.

That's why it's so important to stay in touch with what wealth means to you – and to ask yourself whether you might have *already* achieved it. It's up to you to reflect honestly on the progress you've made and the rewards you've gained, and decide for yourself whether they are enough.

In making that decision, you'll probably compare yourself to other people in an effort to measure your success. But comparisons have a dark side as well as a light side. Some help and empower you, while others hold you back.

The very worst perspective is a superficial, one-dimensional comparison on the basis of material wealth. If you see money merely as a way of keeping score, you will never win the game – because there will always be someone who is better off than you.

If you don't believe me, just listen to legendary investor Warren Buffett. 'If you have a hundred thousand dollars and you think a million is going to make you happy, it's not going to happen,' he says. 'You will look around and see people with two million dollars. It doesn't work that way.' [8]

I'm not just talking about business leaders or celebrities whose lives are obviously distant from yours, but the people you see every day. People like neighbours with better cars, family members who take longer holidays or friends with more beautiful homes.

If you insist on comparing yourself with people who are better off, you soon fall into 'compare and despair', which is a mindset of envy, frustration and lack of fulfilment. You get pulled away from your own idea of wealth, and into someone else's. Instead of working towards what you *could* achieve, you start striving for something that someone else may have, but you probably can't. At that point, you are no longer living, but 'being lived'.

If you must compare yourself with others, focus on those who are worse off than yourself. Not in an arrogant or gloating way, but with a sense of gratitude and humility. You probably won't have to go far outside your front door before you see someone who'd be happy with a tenth of what you have.

---

[8] Zameena Mejia, 'Billionaire Warren Buffett: Doubling your net worth won't make you happier', CNBC, 20 March 2018.

Even better, judge your wealth against your *own* ideals. Go back to the vision you created in chapter 2 and check how far you've come. Alternatively, remember your younger self, and see yourself through their eyes. What would 'past you' think of 'present you'? What would they say, if they could see you now?

When you think about it, just creating and building a freelance business is a huge achievement in itself. There was probably a time when you doubted whether you could do it at all. Yet, here you are.

Or you can go further back than that. In my 20s, I spent several years just drifting, doing temp jobs and messing about with music. I don't regret that time, but I have to admit that I had no ambition, no direction, no real sense of my future at all. If someone had told me that I would enjoy the lifestyle I have now, without even having a full-time job, I would have been amazed.

We *all* need to hang on to that sense of wonder about our lives. Don't let familiarity breed contempt. Instead, cultivate an 'attitude of gratitude'.

Sometimes, we have to open our eyes to the everyday. In 2014, Holly Aston, a young student journalist working at the local newspaper *Peterborough Today*, posted her review of Pizza Express.[9] For most diners, Pizza Express is a reliable old favourite rather than an exhilarating thrill-ride or a voyage of culinary discovery. Indeed, it's so familiar that it scarcely merits a review. But Holly (and her mum, who went along) were bowled over. 'My first reaction was "wow",' she wrote. 'We started eating and it tasted absolutely amazing…'

---

[9] Pizza Express is a mid-market UK pizza chain, similar to Olive Garden or California Pizza Kitchen in the US. The actual review is no longer online, but you can read part of it at https://www.huffingtonpost.co.uk/2014/09/19/work-experience-girls-pizza-express-review-is-totally-utterly-awesome_n_5849260.html

The review went viral, being widely shared and commented on by haters and fans alike. The cynics couldn't believe that a reputable newspaper had published such a naïve, credulous piece. But for many others, Holly's enthusiasm and unworldliness were a delight.

I'm in the second camp. The things we enjoy every day *are* absolutely amazing. That is the right understanding of our lives. If we can't see that, or if we deny it, that says more about us than it does about the world. Instead of constantly trying to improve the quality of our lives, we should be trying to enhance our awareness. Or at least, we need to balance ambition on one hand with appreciation on the other. Otherwise we will be forever travelling, but never arrive.

It might sound like I'm undermining the core message of this book. But I'm not saying you should give up everything and go and live in a cave, wearing a hessian vest and eating wild berries. I'm just pointing out that when wealth arrives for you, it will not come with a flash of lightning and a trumpet fanfare. Instead, you'll look at everything you've done in your freelance life, all the goals you've achieved and the all rewards you've gained, and you'll realize that they're enough.

I wish you the very best of luck.

Please review!

If you found this book valuable, please take five minutes to write a positive review on Amazon.
It would mean a lot to me, and it will help more freelancers like you discover the book.
Thank you!

About the author

Tom Albrighton has been a freelance copywriter for over 12 years.

In that time, he's written about everything from cupcakes and cameras to spectacles and solar panels, working for household names like Prudential, Jeyes and Fuji, as well as dozens of small businesses and marketing agencies.

Tom was an original co-founder of ProCopywriters, the UK alliance of commercial writers. In a 2015 DMA survey, he was ranked the #7 'Copywriter rated by copywriters'.

His other books are *Copywriting Made Simple* and *The Freelance Introvert* (see overleaf).

By the same author

COPYWRITING MADE SIMPLE

How to write powerful and persuasive copy that sells

★★★★★
'Excellent'

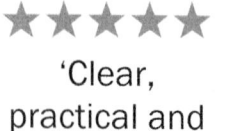

★★★★★
'This book is gold'

★★★★★
'So easy to read'

★★★★★
'Clear, practical and encouraging'

★★★★★
'I love this book'

★★★★★
'Buy it!'

By the same author

Copywriting is writing with purpose. It's about using words to reach people and change what they think, feel and do.

This easy-to-read guide will teach you all the essentials of copywriting, from understanding products, readers and benefits to closing the sale.

It's packed with real-life examples that will show you exactly how the ideas and techniques will work in the real world.

Plus there's a whole chapter of handy tips on writing ads, websites, broadcast media, direct mail, social media and print.

What you'll learn…

- Understand the **product** and its **benefits**
- Get to know your **reader**
- Decide how your copy will change how the reader **thinks, feels or acts**
- **Talk to your reader** and make your copy more like a conversation
- **Bring the product to life** with rich, sensory language
- Learn eight proven formulas for **enticing headlines**
- Choose a rock-solid **structure**
- Create powerful **calls to action**
- Use 20 proven strategies for **creative copy**
- Make **persuasion and psychology** work for you
- Create a unique **tone of voice** for a brand.

Copywriting Made Simple is the perfect introduction to copywriting today.

Find it on Amazon in paperback, ebook or audiobook, or learn more at **copywritingmadesimple.info**

By the same author

THE FREELANCE INTROVERT

WORK THE WAY YOU WANT WITHOUT CHANGING WHO YOU ARE

★★★★★
'This book changed my life'

★★★★★
'Insightful, easy to read and very enjoyable'

★★★★
'Loved this book… made me excited about the future'

★★★★★
'Great eye-opener'

★★★★★
'I felt it was written about me'

★★★★★
'Excellent book'

By the same author

Are you an introvert?

If you're happy in your own company most of the time, have just a few close friends and prefer to work alone, the answer is probably yes.

Modern working styles can be really hard on introverts. Freelancing offers a way out – but it also takes work. To make a success of it, you'll need to learn some new skills, overcome some challenges and build your confidence.

The Freelance Introvert shows you how to create and manage your freelance business, from taking the first steps to time management, working with clients and marketing.

What you'll learn…

- Why introversion is a strength, not a weakness
- How to decide what you want from freelance life
- How to find the right clients… and avoid the wrong ones
- How to set prices without self-sabotaging
- How to manage your time and set boundaries
- How to break through self-limiting beliefs.

Find *The Freelance Introvert* on Amazon in paperback, ebook and audiobook.

Printed in Great Britain
by Amazon